Programming in Igor Pro

A Comprehensive Introduction

Martin Schmid

Copyright 2018 by Martin Schmid – All rights reserved
All rights reserved. No part of this publication may be reproduced, distributed, or transmitted in any form or by any means, including photocopying, recording, or other electronic or mechanical methods, without the prior written permission of the author. While best efforts have been made in preparing this book, the author makes no warranties of any kind and assumes no liabilities of any kind with respect to the accuracy or completeness of the contents and specifically disclaims any implied warranties of merchantability or fitness of use for a particular purpose. The author shall not be held liable or responsible to any person or entity with respect to any loss or incidental or consequential damages caused, or alleged to have been caused, directly or indirectly, by the information contained in this book.
Cover design by Martin Schmid, all rights reserved.

Igor Pro is a product of WaveMetrics, Inc. See www.wavemetrics.com for more information.

About the author:
Martin Schmid (Dr.) is currently pursuing an academic career in the field of surface science. He is using Igor Pro on a daily basis to analyze and visualize spectroscopic data. His professional life led him to Würzburg, Heidelberg, Erlangen, Cambridge (Massachusetts), and Marburg.

The code and text in this book were thoroughly checked for errors. However, any error that was not spotted by the author can be reported at:
erratum_igorbook@freenet.de

PROGRAMMING IN IGOR PRO

PART I

1 FUNDAMENTALS 1

1.1 THE CONTEXT 1
1.2 PROGRAMMING WITH PROCEDURE WINDOW AND COMMAND LINE 2
1.3 USING THE DEBUGGER 6
1.4 DIFFERENT METHODS IN IGOR 7
1.5 CODE LAYOUT 7

2 WRITING MODULES 10

2.1 A SUITABLE LOCATION FOR CODE FILES 10
2.2 THE MODULE-STATIC APPROACH 10
2.3 #INCLUDE STATEMENTS 13
2.4 SHARING YOUR CODE 14

3 WRITING GRAPHICAL USER INTERFACES 15

3.1 CONTROL ELEMENTS AND PANELS 15
3.2 DESIGNING GRAPHICAL USER INTERFACES (GUIs) WITH THE MOUSE 16
3.3 REFINING AN EXISTING GUI 22

PART II

4 FUNCTIONS AND THEIR LOCAL DATA-OBJECTS 27

4.1 FUNCTIONS IN GENERAL 27
4.2 LOCAL AND GLOBAL VARIABLES AND STRINGS IN FUNCTIONS 28
    4.2.1 *Variables and complex variables* *28*
    4.2.2 *Strings* *31*
    4.2.3 *Conversion between strings and variables* *32*
    4.2.4 *Structure variables* *33*
    4.2.5 *Implicitly declared variables and strings* *35*
4.3 REFERENCES TO GLOBAL DATA-OBJECTS 36
    4.3.1 *Operators that work with references to global objects* *37*
    4.3.2 *Conversion of a string into a name/reference with $* *38*
    4.3.3 *Implicit and explicit references* *38*
    4.3.4 *Obtaining wave references from graphs and data folders* *40*

		4.4	Passing parameters 41
		4.4.1	*Pass-by-value and pass-by-reference* 41
		4.4.2	*Optional parameters* 42
		4.5	Flow control in functions 44
		4.5.1	*Decisions* 44
		4.5.2	*Loops* 48

5 GLOBAL DATA-OBJECTS IN IGOR EXPERIMENTS 52

5.1	Global data-objects 52
5.2	Data-objects for storing numbers and characters 53
5.2.1	*Waves* 53
5.2.2	*Global variables and global strings* 61
5.2.3	*Constants and string-constants* 62
5.2.4	*Data folders* 62
5.3	Data-objects that store meta-information 64
5.3.1	*Dependencies* 65
5.3.2	*Structure variable definitions* 65
5.3.3	*Function definitions* 65
5.3.4	*Paths* 66

6 STRINGS, CHARACTERS, AND OUTPUT 66

6.1	Fundamental properties of strings 66
6.2	Handling individual ASCII/Unicode characters 67
6.3	Operations with strings 68
6.3.1	*Analyzing strings with sscanf* 71
6.3.2	*Changing string contents with sprintf* 73
6.3.3	*Escape sequences in strings* 73
6.4	List strings and key-value lists 73
6.4.1	*List strings* 74
6.4.2	*Key-value lists* 75
6.5	Formatted printing 76
6.5.1	*Formatted printing to the command line: printf* 76
6.5.2	*Formatted printing into strings and files* 78
6.6	Regular expressions 78

PART III

7 SPECIAL TOPICS 82

- 7.1 Bit parameters and bit operators...82
- 7.2 Accessing the hard drive...85
  - 7.2.1 Reading and writing files 85
  - 7.2.2 Creating folders on the hard drive 88
- 7.3 Creating a help file 88
- 7.4 Handling errors during runtime 90
- 7.5 The conditional operator "?:" 92
- 7.6 What else is out there? 93

8 SAMPLE PROGRAMS 94

- 8.1 A simple example for structures 95
- 8.2 Storing parameters in strings vs. waves: runtime comparison ...97
- 8.3 Calculating curves #1 99
- 8.4 Calculating curves #2 100
- 8.5 Finding the location of a wave on a graph.................................102
- 8.6 Normalizing spectra/curves in a plot 104
- 8.7 Making an .avi animation 106
- 8.8 A simple genetic algorithm to find a word.................................108
- 8.9 A tool to observe the output of printf 112
- 8.10 A tool to check regular expressions 115
- 8.11 An interactive function plotter..118
- 8.12 A calculator frontend..121
- 8.13 Remote control of Igor with batch files – and remote control of the operating system with Igor via batch files 124
- 8.14 Using a hook function when closing a window.........................126
- 8.15 Using function references 127
- 8.16 A simple neural network for curve fitting.................................129

APPENDIX A GUI CONTROL ELEMENTS 132

APPENDIX B LIST BOX MODES AND BIT PARAMETERS 135

APPENDIX C IGOR VS. OTHER LANGUAGES 138

APPENDIX D FUNCTION DECLARATIONS 140

APPENDIX E USEFUL KEYBOARD SHORTCUTS................... 142

Preface

Igor Pro is a powerful tool for data analysis and visualization in a scientific and engineering context. In addition to many built-in features, Igor also has its own programming language. While this language is not object-oriented, like many modern and popular programming languages, it gives you direct access to a powerful environment for data analysis and visualization. Igor also supports the design of graphical user interfaces. For the scientist or engineer, this can be more valuable than having object-oriented code!
Many of the core concepts of Igor's programming language can also be applied in other programming languages; for example: functions, loops and decision structures, variables and structure variables, regular expressions, bitwise operators, static functions, etc.

The purpose of this book is to present the fundamentals of programming Igor in a comprehensive way, sometimes from a bird's eye view. It is organized into three parts:

Part I comprises the first three chapters and deals with fundamental aspects. In chapter 3, a recipe for a quick and convenient design of graphical user interfaces is provided.

Part II consists of chapters 4 to 6 and provides more in-depth information about the types of data-objects and functions in Igor Pro.

Part III comprises chapters 7 and 8. Chapter 7 contains more practical background information about selected topics. Chapter 8 lists several useful and fully functional code examples.

All programs in this book have been written with Igor Pro 7.08. Some of the programs require Igor Pro 7, or higher versions, and will not work with older versions.

The author wants to thank Joshua E. Klobas, Benedikt P. Klein, and Maik Schöniger for their help during the preparation of this book.

Part I

Fundamentals and Basic Code Design Principles

1 Fundamentals

1.1 The context

While the Igor Pro help files exhaustively explain all details of Igor Pro, this little book should allow you to ease into programming Igor. It is supposed to complement, not substitute, the official manual.
The author assumes that you are somewhat familiar with Igor. If this is not the case, you are strongly advised to take the "Guided Tour of Igor Pro" in chapter I-2 of the official manual (accessible through *Help>Manual* in the menu bar).

An Igor experiment can be thought of as an environment, you could also say "box", for certain data-objects: numeric *variables*, *strings* (character sequences), and *waves* (arrays of data values). Waves can have up to four dimensions and contain numeric values or characters.[1] You can load waves from external sources or create them within the Igor experiment.
It is possible to create subfolders ("smaller boxes") within an Igor experiment, that is, within the experiment's main folder which is called *root*. Like the *root* folder, every subfolder can contain variables, strings, waves, and further subfolders.
The data-objects in an Igor experiment can be viewed with the data browser (Ctrl+B, or Cmd+B on Mac) and Igor offers a large number of methods to manipulate them. The simplest ways of manipulation are displaying a wave in a graph or creating a table with the wave's contents.

---

[1] Waves can also carry meta-information. For example: A numeric wave can carry x-axis scaling information. If the wave contains three values, y={1,4,9}, it is possible to assign corresponding x-values as meta-information, for instance, x={0.5,1,1.5}. The assignment of this specific meta-information is done with the command SetScale.

You are not restricted to stick only to Igor's built-in methods – you can also implement your own methods for specific tasks by writing *programs*. For this purpose, Igor provides a programming language.

A program consists of one or more functions. In order to be useful, most functions must contain internal data-objects. These data-objects are *local*, that is, they are only accessible from within the function and are lost once the function terminates; this is the main criterion which distinguishes them from their permanent *global* counterparts in the "box".

Inside functions, we will always access global data-objects via *local references*. The precise meaning of this statement will become clear in the following chapters.

1.2 Programming with procedure window and command line

Igor provides a command line (Ctrl/Cmd+J) and a procedure window (Ctrl/Cmd+M). These two elements can be combined to write and execute programs. In every Igor program, all instructions have to be encapsulated within a *function*. After calling a function, the sequence of Igor instructions within the function is executed from top to bottom, line by line. The following examples show, in a nutshell, the interplay between command line and procedure window and demonstrate the key features of Igor programming.

If you are a beginner, you should not feel intimidated if some of the code below is not intuitively clear right from the start. Later chapters will explain the details. Further information and helpful details about all commands below can be found in the help files (in the menu bar select *Help>Igor Help Browser>Command Help*).

Example 1 – hello world:
1. Go to *Windows>Procedure Windows>Procedure Window*
   - or -
   use the shortcut Ctrl+M (Cmd+M on a Mac).
2. The procedure window opens up, the "Compile" button is at the bottom center-left.
3. Write a hello world program:
   ```
   function sayHello(word)
       string word
       print "hello " + word    //comment: print to command line
   end
   ```
1. Click on "Compile" and go to the command line (Ctrl/Cmd+J).
2. On the command line, type sayHello("world") **and press enter.**

Example 2 – a simple calculation:
1. Go to the procedure window.
2. Enter the following code:
   ```
   function getRoot ( x, y )
        variable x, y    // first thing: declare parameters
        variable z       // then declare variable
        z = y^(1/x)
        print "x = ", x
        print "y = ", y
        print "y^(1/x) = ", z
        return z
   end
   ```
3. Compile, go to the command line, and enter several pairs of values: for example getRoot(3,8).
4. Execute print getRoot(2,2). What is the difference to getRoot(2,2)?

Example 3 – optional parameters:
1. Go to the procedure window.
2. Enter the following code, which includes optional parameters:
   ```
   function PlotSine(freq,[shift,offset])                                    1)
        variable freq; variable shift; variable offset

        if( ParamIsDefault(shift))    // initialize default values for the   2)
             shift = 0.3*pi           // optional parameters
        endif

        // this is an alternative to the if-construction above,
        // with the ?: operator (conditional operator)
        offset = ( ParamIsDefault(offset) ? 3 : offset)                      3)

        print "frequency = ", freq
        print "shift = ", shift
        print "offset = ", offset

        //further below, the following statements will be explained in detail
        //for now: this is simply how to store values in waves
        make /O /D /N=1000 sineWave    //create a wave                       4)
        wave sW = sinewave             //make a reference
        SetScale /I x 0, 2*pi, sW      //define the x axis range
        sW = offset + sin(freq*(x-shift))
        Display /K=1 sW
   end
   ```
3. Compile, go to the command line, and try:
   - PlotSine(1)

1.2 Programming with procedure window and command line

- PlotSine(1,offset=3)
- PlotSine(1,shift=2,offset=4)
  (optional parameters in user functions always require explicit naming of the parameters)
4. Use the data browser (Ctrl/Cmd+B) to see in which data folder the wave "sineWave" was created.
5. Exercise: Use Igor Pro's help files to understand the meaning of the /K, /O, and /N flags in the code above. For details about make and wave see chapter 5.2.1 (and also 4.3.3).

1) Optional parameters are enclosed in [ ] in the function definition.

2) The function needs to check if an optional parameter was supplied. If not, a suitable default value has to be set. Here, the variable shift is set to 0.3*pi in case the user did not supply a value for shift. ParamIsDefault() checks if the user did not provide a value for the optional parameter.

3) This is an alternative way for 2) with the help of the *conditional operator* "?:" (see page 92 for details).

4) This instruction creates a wave in the *currently active data folder* with 1000 points and *double* numeric precision (/D). Unless you manually created a data folder in the data browser and set it as current data folder (with the red arrow) before running the function, "sineWave" is located in the root folder. /O prevents an error if a wave with the name "sineWave" already exists.
wave creates a local reference ("sW") to "sineWave"; it is scaled with SetScale. The values are assigned via the reference sW, not the wave name "sineWave". Alternatively, you could also write:

   make /O /D /N=1000 sineWave
   sineWave = offset + sin(freq*(x-shift))

using an *implicitly compiler-generated reference* (which has, to add some more potential for confusion, the same name as the wave itself). This is explained in detail on page 38. In this book, implicit references will be avoided; they work only in special cases and can cause confusion. For now, do not use them.

Example 4 – dialogs:
1. Go to the procedure window.
2. Enter the following code:
   ```
   function SaySomething()
       string name
       prompt name, "What's your name?"                                    1)
       DoPrompt "A little question", name    // creates a dialog and
                                             // control variables, such
                                             // as V_Flag, to store input
       if (V_Flag)                                                          2)
           return -1
       endif

       DoAlert 0, "Hello "+ name                                           3)
       return 0
   end
   ```
3. Go to the command line and execute the program.
4. Execute the function in connection with the print command (print SaySomething()) and also use the cancel button on the dialog.

1) Igor offers standard dialogs for user input, these are specified with prompt and invoked by DoPrompt.

2) The variable V_Flag seems to come out of nowhere. This is because it is *implicitly* generated in step 1). Many Igor procedures generate these implicit variables. More details about this topic are given on page 35.
   If the user canceled the DoPrompt dialog, DoPrompt will write a value different from zero into V_Flag. In this case, the if-loop is entered and the program prematurely leaves with the return statement. return has to work with a number. The fact that the function was exited prematurely is indicated by returning a "-1". The full meaning is:
   "If V_Flag has a value different from zero, then use the return statement to leave the function prematurely."

3) Generate a message dialog in case everything went normal. Indicate that everything went normal by returning a zero.

With command line and procedure window, you have powerful tools for programming. Igor's help on programming topics is essentially designed to work on this level.

By default, Igor will insert two #pragma statements (*compiler directives*) at the beginning of every procedure: #pragma rtGlobals and #pragma TextEncoding. They control details of the (compiler's) default behavior; in the remainder of this book, we will just leave them where Igor puts them. Compiler directives are well documented in chapter IV-3 of the manual.

All functions in the procedure window will be saved along with the entire experiment file. They are only available in the .pxp file in which they were created.

1.3   Using the debugger

Igor's built-in debugger allows you to follow the program execution line by line. This tool can be extremely useful for troubleshooting. A small demonstration illustrates how to use it.

1. Bring the procedure window to the front (Ctrl/Cmd+M).
2. Enter the following code into the procedure window – it will produce an error upon execution:

```
function DbgEx()
    wave myData = DataWave
    print myData[0]
end
```

3. Compile the program – there is no compilation error.
4. Go to the command line and execute DbgEx() – and observe the error message.

In the code, we use the keyword wave to generate a local reference to a wave called "DataWave".[2] The error is that this wave does simply not exist, so the local reference points nowhere. How can you find this error with the debugger? This is quite simple:

1. Bring the procedure window to the front (Ctrl/Cmd+M) and activate *Procedure>Enable Debugger*.
2. Go to the procedure window.

---

[2] This is similar to opening a file on the hard drive with a C/C++ program; in this case, you need to generate a *file pointer* inside the function.

3. Generate an entry point by doing a left-click directly in front of the line number – a red dot appears.
4. Execute the program again. This time, the debugger window will open as soon as the program reaches the entry point.
5. Use the button "Step" to execute the program line by line. Error messages will be displayed in the text field on the top right corner of the debugger window.

1.4 Different methods in Igor

Igor knows different types of methods, these are:

- Functions
- Operations

Functions receive their instructions via *arguments* that are passed to them inside parentheses in the function call. Functions usually return values, for example, the results of a numeric calculation or string operation. An example for a function is `UpperStr("aBc")`, which receives the string "aBc" as parameter and returns the string "ABC".

Operations do not receive their instructions via parameters in parentheses, and they usually do not return values. They receive their specifications via command *flags*, which are marked by a slash. The operation `make` is a typical example. The command `make /D /N=1000 TestWave` instructs Igor to make a wave named TestWave, with a length of 1000 points and double precision.

There are, in fact, several more types of user-defined methods. These are: *macros*, *procedures*, and *window-definitions*. However, these constructions are outdated and included in modern Igor versions mostly for backward compatibility. They are ignored in the remainder of this book.

1.5 Code layout

The programming language of Igor is, for the most part, not case sensitive. It does not matter if you write `make`, `Make`, or `MAKE`. There are, however, functions and procedures which distinguish between lower and upper case letters in their arguments. For example: `printf "%e\r", 3000` is different from `printf "%E\r", 3000` (for details on the `printf` command see page 76). Apart from these exceptions, a programmer is free to decide which way of writing the code seems best.

1.5 Code layout

In this book, the choice for upper or lower case characters is guided by readability considerations. WAVE IW is not as easy to read in a long code segment as wave IW. Likewise, SETDATAFODER is harder to read than setDataFolder. In the author's experience, it is a good practice to decide for lower case, upper case, or "camel case"[3] in a flexible way to maximize the readability of the code.

It can help readability to put more than one instruction in one line. In these cases, the instructions have to be separated by a semicolon ";".

The general code layout of programming languages is often determined by certain conventions (style guides). In this book, the code layout was optimized for readability and clarity. After some time, every programmer will develop an individual style, but emphasizing readability and clarity seems to be always a good idea.

Another way of simplifying code is using subroutines. If you use a subroutine, you outsource some of the instructions to a different function. Subroutines also help to highlight the logical structure of code.

```
function mainProg()

    variable a = 4; variable b = 7; variable result

    result = subProg(4,7)
    print "The result is ", result

end

function subProg(A,B)

    variable A      //the variables that the functions receives
    variable B      //have to be declared in the first lines
    variable C

    C = A*B
    return C

end
```

---

[3] "camel case" means mixing upper and lower case characters to improve readability of long words. "setDataFolder" is a typical example.

Exercises

It is highly recommended that you try to solve these exercises.

1.1 Write a program that calculates the diameter of a circle from the circumference. Use DoPrompt and DoAlert. You will possibly need a conversion between strings and numbers; use the functions str2num() and num2str(). Details can be found in Igor's help menu.

1.2 Locate the "Igor Pro User Files" folder on your system. (Hint: have a look in the *Help* menu.)

1.3 Familiarize yourself with Igor's help system – in particular with the filtering options in the "Command Help" (*Help >Command Help*)! Enter different keywords into the search field, e.g., "variable", "datafolder", "string", etc. (If you enter a built-in command in the procedure window or command line and highlight it with the cursor, you can also use the right mouse button, or the shortcut Ctrl+Alt+F1, to navigate to the help entry about this specific command.)

1.4 Write a program that converts a Celsius temperature into Kelvin and Fahrenheit units and prints the results to the command line. The Celsius temperature should be supplied as a parameter to the function. For example: ConvertT(37). Write different subroutines to return the temperature values: Cel2Kel(), Cel2Far(). Similar to the main routine, supply the Celsius temperature as a parameter in each case.
Use $T_{Kel} = 273.15 + T_{Cel}$ and $T_{Fahr} = T_{Cel}*(9/5) + 32$

1.5 Write a program that calculates and displays the following functions:
    a) $\sin(x)/x$ for $\{ x \mid x \geq -2$ and $x \leq 2 \}$
    b) $1 + x + (x^2)/2 + (x^3)/6$ for $\{ x \mid x \geq -10$ and $x \leq 10\}$

1.6 What does the /K=1 flag in example 3 do? What are other options for this flag according to the manual? (Hint: *Help >Command Help* - check also the advanced filtering options.)

2 Writing Modules

2.1 A suitable location for code files

In the previous chapter, the programs were saved inside individual Igor experiment (.pxp) files. Of course, Igor offers the possibility to store code in external files – which makes code re-usage and code-sharing much more convenient.
It is important to realize that there is *one distinct folder* on the hard drive in which code files should be saved! This is Igor's "User Files" folder. It can be easily located through Igor's help menu: select *Help>Show Igor Pro User Files*. This folder contains, amongst others, two subfolders which are important for programming:

- Igor Procedures – contents are *always loaded* when Igor starts up
- User Procedures – contents are *loaded on demand* with #include statements

Where a specific piece of code is saved depends on whether the code should (a) always be available as soon as Igor starts up, or (b) only be loaded on demand.

You can add subfolders in the "Igor Procedures" and "User Procedures" folders. This is regularly done when a *package* is created. A package is a bundle of code, intended to be shared among users (for more details see chapter 2.4). Shortcuts (to external folders) that are saved in "User Procedures" or "Igor Procedures" will be treated as if the external folder would actually be in "User Procedures" or "Igor Procedures".
Code that is saved in "Igor Procedures" will be compiled every time Igor starts up. Code that is saved in "User Procedures" must be called with an #include statement before it can be used; however, in the long run, this can have unwanted side effects. The #include statement and its side effects will be discussed in chapter 2.3.

2.2 The module-static approach

Writing Igor functions in the default way has a significant drawback: it does not prevent name conflicts between different functions which have, by coincidence, the same name. However, you can avoid this situation quite easily by using *modules* and *static functions*. This approach will *encapsulate* the

2.2 The module-static approach

function within the module. If code is written in this way, Igor's syntax actually resembles the syntax of object oriented programming languages like C++.
Here is a first example: we write a small program in modular form. You have to enter the code in a new procedure, <u>not</u> in Igor's procedure window that you call with Ctrl/Cmd+B.

1. In the menu bar, go to *Windows>New>Procedure...*
2. As procedure name use "HelloWorld", the same name as for the module. Choosing a different name is possible, however, this can lead to confusion and errors because Igor does not specifically check for conflicting module names! On the other hand, conflicting procedure file names are easy to detect.
3. In the window that opens up, enter the following code:

```
#pragma moduleName = HelloWorld                                    1)

static function main()                                             2)
    print "Hello World!"
end
```

4. Call the function from the command line: HelloWorld#main()
5. If you want to keep the program, go to *File>Save Procedure As*
6. Navigate to the "Igor Procedures" folder and save it as "HelloWorld.ipf" – now it will be compiled every time Igor starts up.

1) The #pragma instruction allows to declare the module name. It's a compiler instruction like, for example, #include.

2) The keyword static limits the validity of the function to the .ipf file in which it is defined.

There is a strong resemblance to the call of a member function in an object oriented programming language. The operator "." from, e.g., C++ is simply replaced by "#". This approach allows to uniquely identify each function. In this way, an arbitrary number of different modules can have functions with the same names without causing any name conflicts.
The main routine of a module does not have to be named main() – although this is probably a good idea to highlight the code structure. It also makes programs easier to read for C/C++ programmers.

Here is how the approach works:

1. static limits the scope of the function to the current procedure. By default, only functions from the same procedure file/module can call this function. From other files, or the command line, it is invisible.

2. If the module's name is explicitly given in the function call, you can access these hidden functions. The command HelloWorld#main() is interpreted as "look into the module 'HelloWorld' and call its static function 'main()'".

Attention: if the keyword static is omitted, name conflicts are not prevented any more!

If you intend to use a function in more than just one experiment (.pxp) file, you should consider encapsulating the code in a module. If a function will be used only in one experiment file, it is (perhaps) reasonable to use Igor's procedure window (Ctrl/Cmd+M) and the non-static function. The same holds true for quick-and-dirty prototyping, which can also be done in the procedure window.

Using static constants and static structure variables

There are additional data-objects that can be defined within a module: constants, string-constants, and structures variables. The details about these data-objects will be explained in more detail in later chapters. For now, it is only important to know that they can be encapsulated within a module just like functions with the keyword "static".

Independent modules

Modules can be made *independent*, i.e., once they are compiled they are independent of any further compilation issues that may arise with other modules. They basically behave like Igor's built-in functions. For further information, please refer to the Igor Pro manual. Setting a module as independent during the development phase is probably not a good idea, because independent modules cannot be debugged by default. Only after a module is complete and thoroughly checked for errors, it should be saved as an independent module.

2.3 #include statements

If code is saved in the "User Procedures" folder, it will not be automatically available when Igor starts up or an additional instance of Igor is started[4]. To load a procedure file on demand, open the procedure window (Ctrl/Cmd+M) and type:

> #include "Name of the .ipf file without file suffix"

After compilation, the procedure is available.

Of course, you are not restricted to the procedure window if you want to use #include. Every module can contain #include statements to call other modules from the "User Procedures" folder.

In a broader context, #include statements can also be used to load procedures from various locations on the computer, in particular the folder "WaveMetrics Procedures" (go to *Help>Show Igor Pro Folder*). Usually, you will not save your own programs there, however, this folder already contains a large number of additional procedures that could be very useful for you. See the command help for #include for more details.

There are potential disadvantages of #include that become obvious if you imagine the following situation:
You generated a module and used it in many Igor files to analyze data. Every time you did so, you loaded the module with an #include statement in the procedure window. Later on, you decide to share some of your Igor .pxp files with a colleague. However, this colleague does not have the modules. Every time the colleague tries to open one of your .pxp files, error messages by the #include statements show up: they cannot find the modules on your colleagues computer.
Or another situation: After using a module many times in different Igor experiments (and always using #include statements) you decide, for a certain reason, to remove or rename the module. Now, every Igor .pxp file with an include statement to the outdated module name will produce an error during startup.

---

[4] E.g., by selecting *File>Start Another Igor Pro Instance* from the menu bar.

Using #include statements makes sense if code is not written with the module-static approach! Then, name conflicts between functions are not prevented and you possibly want to control at which point which function is included in a .pxp file. You may also encounter other situations in which it is more favorable to load your modules on demand.

> **You should know ...**
> **Every time after you use an #include statement in a .pxp file, this .pxp file has a dependency on the .ipf file which was included. If this .ipf file is absent, also the .pxp file will be affected and an error message is created when the file is opened.**

2.4 Sharing your code

The simplest way to share code with someone else is:

- Packing the .ipf files in a folder.
- Instructing the other person to copy this entire folder into his/her "Igor Procedures" folder.

That's it. You can – of course – use more fancy loading options by using shortcuts and #include statements to manage packages, as described in "Packages" in chapter IV - 10 of the official Igor manual.

Exercises

  2.1 Rewrite the solution to exercise 1.4 in a modular form. The module name should be "CelsiusConverter". As a name for the main function simply choose "main".

3 Writing Graphical User Interfaces

3.1 Control elements and panels

It is possible to use Igor Pro as a framework for the creation of graphical user interfaces (GUIs). The basic window on which control elements (like buttons or pop-up menus) can be placed is called a *panel*. You can generate a panel from the menu bar with *Windows>New>Panel*. After using the shortcut Ctrl/Cmd+T on the panel, to set it in the *tool palette mode*, it is ready for modification!

Usually, the next step is adding control elements via *Panel>Add Control*. The different types of control elements may be divided into three subgroups:

1. Action controls and input
   - Button
   - Check box
   - List box
   - Slider
   - Set variable
   - Pop-up menu
2. Display
   - Value display
   - Title box
3. Grouping
   - Tab control
   - Group box

In addition, Igor allows you to utilize a control type called *custom control*. This type of control element is very flexible, however, it also requires a certain level of programmer's experience.

It is also possible to put control elements on graphs, or to put graphs and tables onto a panel (graphs and tables are, strictly spoken, not control elements).[5]

Once a panel was created, you can save it as a *recreation macro* so it can be easily recovered – at least the geometric information of where which control element is located in which size. Implementing the functionality behind the graphical user interface is a little bit more complex.

---

[5] This can be achieved with the menu which is called by a right-click into the panel area while it is in tool palette mode.

This chapter will demonstrate how graphical user interfaces can be designed with the mouse and how you can implement the functionality behind the interface in a clear way. The approach, which is shown here, rests on a strict separation between code that defines the geometric properties and code that implements the functionality. Importantly, the geometric information will be coded inside a function, not a macro (in contrast to Igor's default behavior!). Also changing an existing GUI is greatly simplified by this approach.[6]

3.2   Designing graphical user interfaces (GUIs) with the mouse

In this section, we will create a panel with a button that plots a sine wave and a button to close the panel. The most important point is that we will separate the geometrical layout of the user interface from the functions behind the control elements. Therefore, we will proceed in three steps:

1. Write a setup-function that:
    a. Checks if a panel with the same name is already open, and if so, brings this panel to the front and prevents any further steps.
    b. Calls a function that draws the interface and all control elements: draw()
    c. Calls a function that implements the functionality behind the individual elements in the user interface: init()
2. Implement the geometry by:
    a. Using the mouse to draw a user interface and its elements.
    b. Storing the geometrical information in a recreation macro.
    c. Using copy-and-paste to get the content from the recreation macro into the function draw().
3. Implement the functionality of the user interface in the function init().

Later on in this chapter, we will need several global data-objects to implement the GUI functionality: a wave, a global variable, and a data folder. When we create these objects, we will be as specific as possible about the location of these objects within the Igor experiment; we will use the *subfolder syntax* with the operator ":" (see also chapter 5.2.4) to unmistakably identify each object.

---

[6] Of course you can still stick to Igor's default way of creating graphical interfaces. In this case, there is no strict separation between code for geometry and functionality. This way of creating user interfaces is explained in the Igor manual in great detail.

Step 1 – setting up the functions:

#pragma moduleName = MyPanel

static function call()

DoWindow TestPanel	//this will write "1" into V_Flag if //window is open already	1)
if (V_Flag)		2)
DoWindow /F TestPanel	//if it is already open, bring it to front	3)
return -1	//and leave without doing anything else	4)

endif
draw()
init()

end

static function draw()

NewPanel /N=TestPanel /W=(75,45,270,180) as "Panel Caption"	5)

end

static function init()

end

1) The command DoWindow controls various aspects of individual windows. It can, for example, bring a window to the front, delete or hide a window. Here, without a control flag, it serves to determine if a window named "TestPanel" exists in the active experiment; if it does not exist, the variable called V_Flag is set to zero. This variable is *implicitly* defined by DoWindow. See chapter 4.2.5 for more details on this type of variable.

2) Here, the program verifies the content of V_Flag. If V_Flag is set to a value different from zero (because DoWindow determined that a window with the name "TestPanel" already existed) the if-loop is entered.
If V_Flag is zero, DoWindow determined that the window "TestPanel" does not yet exist, the if-loop is omitted, and the program continues as intended.

3) DoWindow is used again, now with the Flag /F. This brings the window "TestPanel" to the front.

4) The return statement causes the immediate exit from the function. return always requires a return-number, which can serve as indicator for the reason why the function exited. Usually, return 0 is used if everything went as planned and return -1 if the function had to exit prematurely.

5) Create the panel with the command NewPanel directly from the code.

You should know ...
The specification of the size, here /W=(75,45,270,180), does not give identical results on every computer. The specific screen resolution of your device and the graphics specifications under *Misc>Miscellaneous Settings...* will have an influence on the geometry. You will probably have to modify the numbers in the /W flag, so that the panel and control elements will fit nicely to your screen.

Setting up the functions is finished; now, we will proceed with setting up the geometrical layout.

Step 2 – designing the geometry of the user interface:

Go to Igor's command line (Ctrl/Cmd+J) and create the panel by executing

MyPanel#call()

This will result in the creation of the following raw user interface.

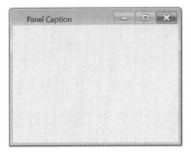

3.2 Designing graphical user interfaces (GUIs) with the mouse

Adjust the size and position of the panel so that it fits best to your screen size and resolution. The appearance of panels and control elements will be affected by the specific screen resolution of your device!

Add the buttons with the following steps:

1. Highlight the panel by clicking on it and use Ctrl/Cmd+T to activate the tool palette for the window.
2. Go to *Panel>Add Control>Add Button ...*
3. Name the button "CalcBut" and set its title to "Calculate"
4. Add another button named "ExitBut" with the title "Close"

Now, the GUI should look like this:

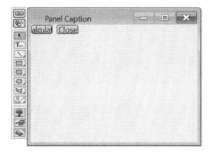

Use the mouse to bring the two buttons in shape and exit the tool palette mode by pressing Ctrl/Cmd+T once again. The result should look like this:

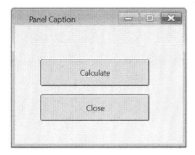

In order to get the code for the panel geometry into the function draw(), we have to make a recreation macro of this window and copy its contents into the function draw(). Make sure, the tool palette is off.

1. Right-click into the panel and select *Form Recreation Macro*
2. Choose an arbitrary name, e.g., by adding the suffix "Temp" to the name suggested by Igor
3. Select the *Create Window Macro* checkbox
4. Press *Do it*
5. Go to the recreation macro by bringing up the procedure window (Ctrl/Cmd+M). There, you should see the following code:

```
Window TestPanelTemp() : Panel
    PauseUpdate; Silent 1       // building window...
    NewPanel /W=(75,45,270,180) as "Panel Caption"
    Button CalcBut,pos={31.50,39.00},size={123.50,30.00},title="Calculate"
    Button ExitBut,pos={30.50,79.50},size={126.00,30.00},title="Close"
EndMacro
```

In a final step, copy and paste the relevant code into the function draw(). Do not copy PauseUpdate; Silent 1. Insert /N=TestPanel.

```
static function draw()

    NewPanel /N=TestPanel /W=(75,45, 270,180) as "Panel Caption"
    Button CalcBut,pos={30.00,39.00},size={126.00,30.00},title="Calculate"
    Button ExitBut,pos={30.00,79.50},size={126.00,30.00},title="Close"

end
```

Important: Now close the modified panel without saving. Delete the recreation macro TestPanelTemp() from the procedure window to avoid confusion later on! At this point, the interface design is complete.

Step 3 – implementing the functionality of the control elements:

In the final step, the functionality will be implemented. This will be achieved in the function init(). There, add the following two lines:

```
Button CalcBut, win=TestPanel ,proc=MyPanel#CalcFunction
Button ExitBut, win=TestPanel ,proc=MyPanel#Exit
```

With these lines we make the connections between the control elements and the functions behind them. (The first comma directly after the name of the button is optional.)

Next, we implement the functions behind the buttons: CalcFunction() and Exit(). Here, you might wonder why a special *exit* function for closing the window is necessary. After all, the window can be closed by the "cross-button" in the title bar already. The reason is that we will create other data-objects associated with the panel later on, and we want the exit function to delete those objects as well. After closing our panel, Igor should be back to its original state. The "cross-button" in the title bar cannot deal with this requirement (unless you use hook-functions, an advanced programming concept shown on page 126).

To complete the program, we add the following two functions[7] to the module, again as static. We specify explicitly that we want the wave in the root data folder of the experiment file by using subfolder syntax and the operator ":".

```
static function CalcFunction(ctrlName):ButtonControl

    string ctrlName

    make /D /N=1000 /O root:sineWave    //create a wave in the root folder
    wave sw = root:sineWave              //make a local reference
    SetScale /I x, 0, 2*pi, sw
    sw = sin(x)
    display /K=1 sw

end

static function Exit(ctrlName):ButtonControl

    string ctrlName
    DoWindow /K TestPanel                //kills the panel

end
```

Both button control functions expect to receive a string parameter that is called "ctrlName". The functions for other types of control elements require different parameters (see Appendix A).

---

[7] Later on, the details of all functional elements will be discussed in more detail. The specifier :ButtonControl is not mandatory, however, you can keep it to keep the code clear.

In a final step, /K=2 is added into draw() to deactivate the "cross button" in the title bar.

NewPanel /N=TestPanel /K=2 /W=(75,45,270,180) as "Panel Caption"

Now, the exit button remains the only possible way of closing the program. In this way, we will ensure in the following chapter that nothing is "left over" after the panel is closed. Note that you can still use the cross-button in the title bar to close the window if you click it *quickly, five times* in a row.

At this point, the fully functional panel is finished and can be called from the command line (Ctrl/Cmd+J) with MyPanel#call().

> **Igor offers an alternative, and much more flexible, way for the implementation of control element functions by using "structure variables" (chapter 4.2.4). The gain in flexibility comes with a price: writing graphical user interfaces becomes an advanced technique then. The way of implementing control elements shown in this chapter follows an older, but simpler, approach, so that also programmers with less experience can write user interfaces. However, with increasing experience you should focus on the method with structure variables (see the examples in chapter 8 as well as chapter III-14 in the official manual for more information).**

3.3 Refining an existing GUI

Here, we will briefly cover how to improve GUIs in an efficient way. We will take advantage of the separation between geometry and functionality that we implemented it in the previous section.

Here is what we want to achieve:

1. The user is supposed to enter a frequency via a *set variable* element.
2. The value of the frequency is transferred into a *global variable* "SineFrequency", which is linked to the set variable element. The global variable is saved inside a data folder (subfolder in the root folder of the experiment).
3. The function CalcFunction() will then access this global variable and plot a sine wave with the desired frequency.

3.3 Refining an existing GUI

As a preparation, you have to temporarily remove the /K=2 instruction from the code again. It would generate some unnecessary complications in the following steps. After this is done, invoke the *panel geometry* with MyPanel#draw().

Now, use Ctrl/Cmd+T to put the panel into the tool palette mode and add a set variable element with *Panel>Add Control>Add Set Variable*. As a name, use "setFrequency". Use the mouse to bring the elements into shape and position. In the end, we want the final result to look like this:

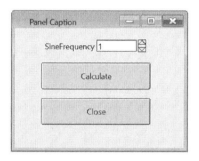

After all elements have been positioned correctly, use Ctrl/Cmd+T again to leave the tool palette mode of the panel; then, use the right mouse button in the panel area, select "Form Recreation Macro", and choose "Create Window Macro". For the recreation macro name use "temp" as a prefix or suffix.

Use Ctrl/Cmd+M to navigate to the recreation macro and copy the code into the function for drawing. Insert the missing /N=TestPanel immediately behind the command NewPanel.

static function draw()

    NewPanel /N=TestPanel /W=(75,45,270,180) as "Panel Caption"
    Button CalcBut,pos={30.00,39.00},size={126.00,30.00},title="Calculate"
    Button ExitBut,pos={30.00,79.00},size={126.00,30.00},title="Close"
    SetVariable setFrequency,pos={34.00,13.50},size={117.50,14.00}

end

Now, delete the recreation macro from the procedure window and close the panel with the cross-button. If the /K=2 flag would still be active, you would have to click the cross-button quickly several times in a row.

23

3.3 Refining an existing GUI

In the next step, we will implement the functionality behind the set variable element. To do so, we will add some additional lines to init(), which will then look like this:

```
static function init()

    Button CalcBut, win=TestPanel ,proc=MyPanel#CalcFunction
    Button ExitBut, win=TestPanel ,proc=MyPanel#Exit
    NewDataFolder /O root:PanelGlobals           //create a subfolder in root
    Variable /G root:PanelGlobals:SineFrequency = 1
    SetVariable setFrequency, win=TestPanel ,value=root:PanelGlobals:SineFrequency

end
```

We use the commands NewDataFolder and Variable /G to create a data folder that contains a global variable called "SineFrequency"; you can inspect both objects in the data browser (Ctrl/Cmd+B). Note the use of ":" to specify the *path* to the global variable in the data browser. The value that we store in "SineFrequency" will be used by CalcFunction() later on. The value= ... instruction of the SetVariable command takes care that the value of the set variable element is directly linked to "SineFrequency". Now, CalcFunction() has to be modified to work with "SineFrequency".

```
static function CalcFunction(ctrlName):ButtonControl

    string ctrlName
    NVAR frequency = root:PanelGlobals:SineFrequency

    make /D /N=1000 /O root:sinewave    //create a wave in the root folder
    wave sw = root:sineWave             //make a local reference
    SetScale /I x, 0, 2*pi, sw

    sw = sin(frequency*x)               //use the reference for value assignment

    display /K=1 sw

end
```

The keyword "NVAR" is used to access the global variable inside the function: a local reference to a global data-object.

Finally, Exit() will take care of deleting the data folder "PanelGlobals" when you close the program.

3.3 Refining an existing GUI

```
static function Exit(ctrlName):ButtonControl

    string ctrlName
    DoWindow /K TestPanel
    KillDataFolder /Z root:PanelGlobals

end
```

When all editing is done, do not forget to re-enter the /K=2 instruction:

```
NewPanel /N=TestPanel /K=2 /W=(261,148,459.5,282) as "Panel Caption"
```

The modified panel is now ready for testing.

> **You should know ...**
> An advanced alternative for the "close-and-clean-button approach" is to use a *hook function* on the panel. This is demonstrated in the code example in chapter 8.14.

Summary

In this chapter, we have learned how to create graphical user interfaces with Igor. There are a few key points that you should keep in mind:

1. Use the module-static approach to encapsulate the code.
2. The interface geometry and functionality can be defined in two separate functions. In this way, it is relatively easy to modify the interface layout, without having to worry about the rest of the code.
3. Elements in Igor's graphical interfaces communicate with each other via global variables. Store these variables in specific data folders and delete these folders when the panel closes (unless you have good reasons to keep them). For more details about global variables and data folders see chapter 5.

Because this book focuses on the big picture and not on details, we will not discuss the individual control elements any further at this point. If you are interested in this topic, you should study the GUI examples in chapter 8 that demonstrate the implementation of graphical user interfaces, as well as appendices A and B. You can also find several interesting cases in *File>Example Experiments*.

> **You should know ...**
> When you share graphical user interfaces with other users, you should consider making them flexible enough to adapt their geometries to different screen resolutions. This can be done with if-else or switch-case-structures in connection with the command "ScreenResolution".
> In particular the treatment of 96 dpi differs from all other screen resolutions. More details about this topic can be found here (via the command line): DisplayHelpTopic "Control Panel Resolution on Windows".

Exercises

3.1 Write a graphical user interface for the temperature converter from Celsius to Fahrenheit. The Celsius temperature is entered via a set variable element. There should be a "close" and a "calculate" button. The Fahrenheit and Kelvin temperatures are displayed on *title box* elements (see also the example in chapter 8.9). Use the Cel2Kel() and Cel2Far() functions from the previous exercises.

3.2 Study the GUI examples in chapters 8.9 - 8.12. You will probably not understand everything at this point. In this case, continue reading the next chapters and return to the examples in your own time.

Part II

Functions and Data-Objects in Igor Pro

Writing Igor procedures has nearly exclusively one goal: analyzing, creating, or changing data-objects such as waves, variables, or strings with appropriate functions. In this part of the book, functions and their internal data-objects are discussed in more detail.

4 Functions and Their Local Data-Objects

4.1 Functions in general

Functions are the fundamental building blocks of programs. They serve as containers for Igor code and can actively receive and return data-objects, usually numeric variables or strings. (In Igor 8, functions can actually return multiple values.) The data-objects that are handed over to functions are called *parameters*. Appendix D provides examples for functions with different combinations of return values and parameters.

Functions can be made *private* to the containing file/procedure window if they are declared with the keyword static.

It is possible to associate functions with certain subtypes, i.e., a function may be identified, for example, with a button on a graphical user interface by writing :ButtonControl directly behind the function's name (see: "Procedure Subtypes" in the Igor manual for further information). Such an association is, however, not mandatory.

Functions can be called by a user from the command line, or from other functions.

Functions have various local (that is, internal) types of data-objects to store information:

1. Local variables and strings
2. Structure variables (short: *structures*)

3. References to global data-objects:
    a. Waves
    b. Global variables, global strings
    c. Data folders
    d. Functions (advanced concept)

In addition, functions can directly access certain other global data-objects without needing a reference: constants and string-constants (page 62), paths (page 66), dependencies (page 65), and, of course, other functions.

4.2 Local and global variables and strings in functions

Local variables are variables that exist inside a function, they cannot be accessed by a different function and they only exist during the runtime of the function.
Global variables are variables that exist parallel to waves and data folders in the Igor experiment. They can be accessed from various functions and they are permanent data-objects.
A *string* is a data-object that can store character sequences. Also strings exist either as local or global strings.
Local *arrays* of strings and variables can be implemented as *free waves*, see chapter 5.2.1 for more details.

4.2.1 Variables and complex variables

Igor provides a standard data type for storing numeric values: variables. The command variable is used to create these data-objects. With version 7, the Igor Pro developers included additional numeric data types that differentiate, for instance, between integer (int) and double (double) precision numbers. However, the standard data type variable creates a variable with double precision as well, so there is a certain degree of redundancy. Regardless of the new numeric subtypes introduced in version 7, you are in most practical cases on the safe side if you stick to the traditional numeric type variable! Therefore, this book will only deal with this type. (For larger integer numbers, the 64 bit variable types int64/uint64 can be better).
Variables can either be real or complex. By default, they are interpreted as real, but if the flag /C is used, they are interpreted as complex[8]. In this case, you have to use the function cmplx() when initializing the variable.

---

[8] *Real* and *complex* in the mathematical sense.

4.2 Local and global variables and strings in functions

Global variables are defined by the flag /G. If they are accessed in a function, you have to create a local reference in the function by using the keyword NVAR. In the following table, the global variables are specified with their absolute path in the Igor experiment (this is the most general way of accessing them).

variable a=2	A local variable.
variable /G root:a=2 NVAR A=root:a	A global variable requires a local reference (created by NVAR) so that the variable can be used inside a function.
variable /C z=cmplx(1,2)	A local complex variable.
variable /G /C root:z=cmplx(1,2) NVAR /C Z=root:z	A global complex variable also requires a local reference.

Igor has various operators that act on variables. The most important ones are listed in the table below. There, operators that can change values of variables are highlighted in bold font, and operators that compare two variables are highlighted in italics.

=	**Assignment**	+=	**Add and assign**	==	*Check equality*
+	**Addition**	-=	**Subtract and assign**	!=	*Check inequality*
-	**Subtraction**	*=	**Multiply and assign**	>	*Greater than*
/	**Division**	/=	**Divide and assign**	>=	*... or equal*
*	**Multiplication**	&&	Logical AND	<	*Smaller than*
^	**Raise to power**	||	Logical OR	<=	*... or equal*
		!	Logical NOT		

The module below demonstrates the use of these operators. The comparison and logical operators return 0 if the statement/result is negative, and 1 otherwise. For complex numbers, you can test equality by the function cequal() – the equality test operator "==" gives an unexpected result.

```
#pragma moduleName = OperatorDemo

static function main()

    variable a, b, c, d, e        //variable declaration
```

4.2 Local and global variables and strings in functions

```
variable m = 0              //variable declaration and initialization
variable n = 1
variable /C z1 = cmplx(0,1)
variable /C z2 = cmplx(1,1)

//demonstrate precision of numbers with printf (see: formatted printing)
printf "%.20f \r", 0.2 + 0.1     //ideally exactly 0.3

// do operations
a = 2 + 1
b = 2 * a
c = b / 3
d = 2*(c - a)
e = 2^a     //2 to the power of a

print "a, b, c,  d, e,   z1,   z2"
print  a, b, c, d, e, z1, z2

a += 1   // short form of a = a + 1
b -= 1
c *= 2
d /= 2
e ++    // another short form e = e + 1
z1 += cmplx(2,4)
z2 *= 2

print a, b, c, d, e , z1, z2," after increment operators"

print "\n applying comparison operators"   //   \n for line break
print a <= b
print c >= d
print e != a
print a > b
print a < b
print a == b
print " ... on complex numbers"
print z1, "==", z2, " -> ", z1 == z2
print "cequal(z1,z2) -> ", cequal(z1,z2)

print "\n applying logical operators"
print m && n
print m || n
print !m

end
```

30

You should play with this function to familiarize yourself with the operators! The operators have a different relative strength (*precedence*): 8^1/3 gives a different result than 8^(1/3)!
In addition, there are also several operators for binary operations/binary numbers. These are explained in chapter 7.1 on page 82.

Igor offers a great number of built-in functions that work with variables. To get an overview, open *Help>Command Help*, select *Advanced Filtering*, and activate the checkbox *Functions*. These functions include, for example, real() or imag(), to obtain the real and imaginary parts of complex numbers.

Apart from numbers, variables can also store values for infinity (INF and –INF) and "not any number" (NaN). As a matter of fact, functions which do not have an explicit terminal return statement actually return NaN. You can check if a variable contains a regular numeric value, +/-INF, or NaN with the function numtype(). Comparison operators do not work with NaN.

4.2.2 Strings

Igor provides a data type for storing character sequences: strings (created with the command string). Strings are at least as important as numeric variables for programming. For this reason, a significant part of chapter 6 is dedicated to them. At this point, only a brief overview is given. The table below shows how strings are declared and initialized.

string word="hello"	A local string
string /G root:word="world" SVAR WORD = root:word	A global string requires a local reference in order to be usable in a function (keyword SVAR).

Non-keyboard characters in strings
On a fundamental level, a computer does not know characters but only numbers. In order to associate numbers with characters, computers use encoding schemes, like ASCII or Unicode. Igor 7 internally uses a UTF-8 encoding scheme, which includes regular ASCII characters, but also a great number of special characters. UTF-8 characters are commonly identified with their hexadecimal numerical code. For instance: 00B5 represents the µ

character.[9] You can use these hexadecimal representations in strings with the *escape sequence* \u; in this way you can initialize the string also with characters that are not available on your keyboard layout. For example: print "\u00B5" prints a μ character.

Operators that act on strings: +, =, +=, []
Strings have much fewer operators than variables; there are, on the other hand, many functions that work with strings (see chapter 6). Strings recognize the assignment operator "=" and the concatenation operator "+".

```
string word = "Hello " + "World"
word += "!"; print word
print word[3]
```

4.2.3 Conversion between strings and variables

The conversion between strings and variables is straightforward, at least if you do not require high accuracy. There are a few standard methods to perform the conversions:

Method	Application
num2str(<number>)	converts a number into a string
num2istr(<number>)	round to nearest integer then convert into a string
str2num(<string>)	convert a string into a number

The numeric precision is somewhat limited, as demonstrated by the following module.

```
#pragma moduleName = StrgNumbConv

static function main()

    variable a; variable b
    string word
    a=1.23456789
    word = num2str(a); print word
    b=str2num(word); print "Error due to inaccuracy: ", b-a

end
```

---

[9] You can easily find a full list of all UTF-8 characters online.

For higher accuracy, you should use the methods sprintf and sscanf; both are explained in chapter 6.3.

If a number has to be interpreted as ASCII code (or vice versa), use the functions num2char() and char2num(). Try print num2char(75) on the command line.

4.2.4 Structure variables

Igor also recognizes a special type of data-object: *structure variables*. A structure variable (short: *structure*) results from merging a set of variables or strings into a new, customized type of data-object. The individual variables or strings are called *members* of the structure. In modules, structures can, and probably should, be declared as static to avoid name conflicts.

A structure variable definition is a blueprint for a new type of data-object. This definition is a global object, while a structure variable is a local data-object! [10]

The syntax for structures is practically identical to the corresponding syntax in C and deviates from the regular Igor syntax! The main differences are the usage of the *member access operator* "." and the possibility of creating arrays in a C-like manner. The following program will demonstrate these points.

```
#pragma moduleName=StructExample

///////////// definition of structure and corresponding functions

static structure ValueSet

    variable value1         //these are the members of the structure
    string word1
    variable values[10]     // this is a C-like array,

endstructure
//manipulate the contents of the structure

static function valueSetOperations(s)

    struct ValueSet &s      // operator "&" for call-by-reference
```

---

[10] While a *blueprint* for your kitchen can be public (global), the kitchen itself is usually private (local).

```
    s.value1 += 1           // here the operator "." is used as in C
    s.word1 += " again"
    s.values[0] += 1

end

/////////// main routine

static function main()

    struct ValueSet myFirstSet    // create a structure data-object

    //initialize the values
    myFirstSet.value1 = 10
    myFirstSet.word1 = "hello"
    myFirstSet.values[0] = 1

    print myFirstSet.value1       // again, pure C syntax
    print myFirstSet.word1
    print myFirstSet.values[0]
    print myFirstSet.values[1]

    //modify the structure
    valueSetOperations(myFirstSet)

    print "modified"
    print myFirstSet.value1
    print myFirstSet.word1
    print myFirstSet.values[0]
    print myFirstSet.values[1]

end
```

You have to keep one point in mind: the function will receive the structure *by reference* and not *by value* (see page 41 for more details). If the function makes changes to the structure's members, it will change the original structure and not only a local copy inside the function. This *passing by reference* is also encountered when a wave reference is passed to a function.

A popular use for structures is to replace global variables, for instance with fit functions. For this purpose, the corresponding structure must stick to a few formal criteria. There is a very instructive example in the Igor Pro manual on page III-229 (topic: structure fit functions).

Notably, structures can also contain members different from strings, variables, and arrays. They support additional data-objects which are equivalent to C data-objects. Details can be found in the Igor help files.

Igor does not only allow generating user-defined structures, it also comes with a set of specific predefined structures. Two important examples are "point" and "rect".

> **You should know ...**
> There are also several built-in structure definitions for control elements on graphical user interfaces. Using structures for control elements is, however, a somewhat advanced technique. These structures are listed in Appendix A.

4.2.5 Implicitly declared variables and strings

Implicitly declared variables cannot be generated by a programmer – they are created by (a large number of) Igor's built-in commands. Consider the following code:

```
#pragma moduleName = ImplicitVar

function main()

    GetFileFolderInfo/Z "C:"           //On Mac: "Macintosh HD:"
    if(V_Flag == 0 && V_isFolder == 1)
        print "Folder Exists!"
    endif

end
```

This program checks if the folder "C:" does exist on a computer and works just as intended. However, this is somewhat puzzling at a first sight! The variables V_Flag and V_isFolder are nowhere declared with the command variable. They cannot be found in the data browser either. It seems that they came out of nowhere and disappeared again.

On the other hand, if you execute GetFileFolderInfo/Z "C:" on the command line, the data browser will fill with many new global variables and strings, amongst them V_Flag and V_isFolder. On the command line, everything seems to be all right.

It is obviously the case that variables and strings that are created by certain built-in procedures do not need declaration. In this respect, these data-objects behave as if they would appear out of nowhere; they are *implicitly declared* by the compiler. Delete the GetFileFolderInfo command in the program above and the program will not compile at all. The reason is simple: the compiler cannot

find any command that could create V_Flag, so it does not make the implicit declaration.
Igor's built-in procedures follow a certain system of nomenclature for implicit variables and strings: different procedures implicitly declare variables with the same name. The most prominent example is the variable V_Flag, which is used by a large number of procedures to store basic information, e.g., if a certain operation was successful or not.
If you want to know which implicitly declared variables and strings are generated by a specific command, you have to consult the help files, or simply execute the command via the command line and look into the data browser.

The implicit handling of data-objects is not only limited to variables and strings, but also extends to references to waves. This is further explained in the chapter on implicit and explicit wave references on page 38.

4.3 References to global data-objects

All global data-objects will be discussed in chapter 5. At this point, we will only consider the references to global data-objects in functions. The following keywords are used to create these references:

- NVAR for numeric variables
- SVAR for strings
- WAVE for waves
- DFREF for data folders

References are local data-objects in functions. There are, in fact, many Igor functions which do not return a string or variable, but a reference. Also user-defined functions can return these data-objects.
The next module illustrates how to create and access global objects with references.

```
#pragma moduleName = LocalRefs

static function main()

        make /N=1000 /O SampleWave      //no specification of the absolute path with root:
        wave sWave = SampleWave         //use a short and easy reference name

        variable /G SampleVar           //no explicit specification of the location:
        NVAR VarRef = SampleVar         //root: is missing
```

```
    string /G SampleString
    SVAR StrRef = SampleString
    NewDataFolder /O SubFolder
    DFREF sFold = SubFolder          //make a reference

    //check if the reference is valid, i.e., the global object exists
    print WaveExists(sWave)          // 1 as return value means it exists
    print NVAR_Exists(VarRef)
    print SVAR_Exists(StrRef)
    print DataFolderExists("SubFolder") //needs the name or path

end
```

Run this program two times: the first time, while the active data folder is the root data folder, and the second time after changing the active data folder to "SubFolder" (with the red arrow in the data browser). Observe where the data-objects are created in the second run! What would change if you explicitly use make /N=1000 /O root:SampleWave in the code? What are the effects of using the relative paths (that is, the data-object names without a specification of a data-folder or root folder)?

4.3.1 Operators that work with references to global objects

Once a reference to a global string or variable has been created, this reference can be used similar to local strings or variables.

For numeric waves (in contrast to text-waves) the relevant operators are: +, -, /, *, ^, =, *=, +=, -=, /=. When assigning values to a numeric wave, you have to use the wave reference, not the global wave name! In this context, the character "x" is readily interpreted correctly as the variable x when entered in a mathematical expression (like in y=sin(2x) or y=ax+b). The examples on pages 99 and 100 illustrate these ideas.

Because of their importance, the **comparison operations** between two references (either variables, strings, waves, or data folders) are explicitly listed in the next table.

4.3 References to global data-objects

Data-object	Comparison operation
Variable	`==` `cequal(z1,z2)` //for complex numbers
String	`StringMatch(str1,str2)`
Wave	`WaveRefsEqual(w1,w2)` //two wave references, //pointing to the same wave? `equalWaves(w1,w2)` // two different waves, same contents?
Data folder	`DataFolderRefsEqual(dfr1,dfr2)` //two references, pointing to the same data folder?

4.3.2 Conversion of a string into a name/reference with $

The operator $ allows to convert a string into a name for a data-object, e.g., as argument for a reference, or the creation of a new object.

```
string name = "root:AnotherWave"
make /O $name
string VarName = "root:AnotherVariable"
variable /G $VarName = 1
```

This little detail is enormously useful: it allows generating dynamic names in programs!

4.3.3 Implicit and explicit references

Some of Igor's built-in operations provide an implicit creation and assignment of references. This can save coding time, however, at a first glance it looks like these operations break Igor's rules. The instructions

```
make /D testWave
testWave = 2*x
```

work just fine without any reference assignment; the compiler treats them like

```
make /D testWave
wave testWave = testWave
testWave = 2*x
```

This can cause confusion, because variations of this code, for instance introduced by using the operator $, do not work with implicit referencing.

38

Consider the following problem: ten waves should be created within a loop, each wave with a specific name: "testWave_0", "testWave_1", ... , "testWave_9". We use a for-loop (details on page 48) to iterate through the waves. As a solution, we try the following two functions quickly in Igor's procedure window (they are so simple that it is not worth the effort to generate a new module). The first approach makes an attempt without explicit referencing:

```
function WaveIteration1()

    variable i
    string baseName = "testWave_"
    string name
    for (i=0; i<10; i+=1)
        name = baseName + num2str(i)
        make /D /O $name
        $name = i*x        // here is the problem
    endfor

end
```

Trying to compile WaveIteration1() fails! However, the code with explicit references:

```
function WaveIteration2()

    variable i
    string baseName = "testWave_"
    string name

    for (i=0; i<10; i+=1)
        name = baseName + num2str(i)
        make /D /O $name
        wave SlidingReference = $name
        SlidingReference = i*x
    endfor

end
```

works as expected. In every iteration of the for-loop, the wave reference is reassigned to the wave which was just created in this iteration.

For the sake of clarity, the author recommends that you stick to explicit wave references - even if the commands in the code already generate implicit wave references. It is better if you have to remember a few simple and general rules

("Always access a global object by its explicit reference.") instead of having to remember many complex rules ("If a global object is created by make or duplicate, and accessed in the same function as the make or duplicate operation, you do not need a reference in this function, unless you use dynamic names with $.").

4.3.4 Obtaining wave references from graphs and data folders

In practical applications, you probably encounter the problem to uniquely identify a wave on a graph: you need a reference. In this case, you can first get a list string with the names of all curves on the graph with the command TraceNameList, and then use the command TraceNameToWaveRef to get the reference for a specific wave from the list. Sometimes a wave is displayed versus another wave. In this case, a reference to this "x-wave" can be obtained with XWaveRefFromTrace. For images and contour plots similar pairs of functions exist: ImageNameList – ImageNameToWaveRef and ContourNameList – ContourNameToWaveRef.

Alternatively to the sequential call of TraceNameList, TraceNameToWaveRef, and XWaveRefFromTrace, you can also use the function WaveRefIndexed to obtain the references to the waves on a given graph.[11]

If cursors are active on a graph (Ctrl/Cmd+I), you can use the function CsrWaveRef to get a reference to the wave marked with the cursor. If this wave is displayed versus another one, it is possible to get the reference to this "x-wave" with CsrXWaveRef.

If you want to get a reference to the data folder (DFREF) in which a specific wave is stored, you can use GetWavesDataFolderDFR. The simple name of the data folder or its path in the folder hierarchy (as visible in the data browser) can be obtained by GetWavesDataFolder.

Most of these operations work in connection with the list-string methods on page 74. Some of these operations are used in the examples on page 102 and page 105.

---

[11] There is a similar function for waves not on a graph, but in a data folder: WaveRefIndexedDFR. This function can be used to iterate through the waves in a data folder.

4.4 Passing parameters

4.4.1 Pass-by-value and pass-by-reference

Passing a local variable to a function as a parameter actually gives a copy of the local variable to the function. This is called **pass-by-value**. The next example illustrates this:

```
#pragma moduleName = PassByValue

static function master()

    variable a =1
    servant(a)
    print "In master: ", a

end

static function servant(a)

    variable a          //the variable which is received has to be declared
    a += 1
    print "In servant: ", a

end
```

On the other hand, it is also possible to pass a variable *by reference* (**pass-by-reference**). Then, the function is given the address of the variable in the computer's memory and can alter the variable itself. This is achieved by declaring the variable with an ampersand in front of the variable's name.

```
#pragma moduleName = PassByRef

static function master()

    variable a =1
    print "In master (before): ", a
    servant(a)
    print "In master (after) : ", a

end

static function servant(a)

    variable &a    //declaration with ampersand to cause pass-by-reference
    a += 1
```

```
print "In servant: ", a
```

end

Functions that receive variables by reference cannot be called from the command line.

> **You should know ...**
> There are more advanced aspects of functions not included in this book. These are: function overrides, threadsafe functions, or functions which run as background tasks.

4.4.2 Optional parameters

Optional parameters have been already mentioned earlier. At this point, a more detailed discussion will follow.

In general, Igor accepts optional parameters in user-defined functions and built-in functions. Optional parameters can be easily recognized in the code, because they appear in brackets. But there are differences between built-in and user defined functions in how optional parameters are passed on to the function.

User defined function	Built-in function
function demo(a,[b, c])	SortList(listStr[,listSepStr[, options])
demo(2) demo(3,c=2) demo(1,c=2,b=5)	print SortList("a;c;b") print SortList("a;c;b",";") print SortList("a;c;b",";",1)
The order in which the optional parameters are passed to the function is not relevant. *But:* you have to explicitly specify the parameter with the assignment operator "=".	The order is relevant. An explicit assignment with "=" will create an error! Parameters in-between optional parameters cannot(!) be skipped: SortList("a;b;c",1) will generate an error!

If you use optional parameters in a function, you have to provide suitable default values, in case a user does not supply any values for the optional parameters. The following example illustrates how this is achieved (the conditional operator ?: is described on page 92 in more detail):

4.4 Passing parameters

```
#pragma moduleName = OptPar

static function main([a, b, word])

    variable a; variable b; string word;

    //check, if default-values are required

    if (paramIsDefault(a))
        a = pi
    endif

    //use the conditional operator as a shortcut
    //for variables - it does not work with strings

    b = ( paramIsDefault(b) ? 2*pi : b)

    if (paramIsDefault(word))
        word = "hello"
    endif
    print a,b,word

end
```

Optional parameters can be used to increase the flexibility of functions. You could encounter the following situation: A button on a graphical user interface serves to update a graph. However, you want to use the button procedure also from the code, i.e., call it from another function and, in this case, pass on some additional information. The button control function requires that a string with the name of the button is passed on to the function – so the function definition must fulfill this formal criterion. It is not possible to use a function for a button control which does not get exactly one string as parameter. However, you can pass on optional parameters! The table below illustrates this approach (the optional :ButtonControl subtype definition is absent). The function in the right column is fit for use with a button *and* for use from within the code with additional information passed on to it.

Standard (without structures)[12]	With optional parameters
function DoThings(ctrlName) 　string ctrlName 　//code end	function DoThings(ctrlName,[var]) 　string ctrlName 　variable var 　//code end
Call by click on a button and from a function DoThings("noButton")	Call by click on a button and from a function DoThings("noButton",var=3)

4.5 Flow control in functions

After its compilation, every Igor program will execute line by line, from top to bottom. In order to make decisions during the program flow or repeat certain segments of the code, *flow control* structures can be used.

4.5.1 Decisions

Igor offers two types of decision structures:

1. if-else and if-elseif
2. switch-case and strswitch-case

if-else decision structures often use comparison operators (like == or <=) or the logical operators && (AND), || (OR), and ! (NOT) to check if a certain condition is fulfilled or not.

switch-case expressions allow to check if a variable has a certain value – from a limited set of options! Each of these options will cause a different code behavior, which is implemented in the corresponding *case* segment of the code. Once a case branch was entered, the program has to be stopped from entering the following branches – this is achieved with the keyword break. Once it is reached in the program flow, the decision structure is left.

---

[12] There is also the "modern" way of implementing functions for control elements with structure variables. In this case, the string ctrlName is replaced by a corresponding structure data-object. The predefined structure definitions for control elements contain a string "userdata"; this string can be used to pass on additional information.

if-else and if-elseif

The *if-else* decision structure checks if a certain condition is fulfilled (the condition is defined inside parentheses), and if so, the code will proceed to the *if-branch* of the structure. If not, the code inside the *else-branch* of the structure will be executed.

The else-branch can contain further, nested if-structures. For this case, Igor allows to use the keyword "elseif".

```
#pragma moduleName = ControlFlow

static function IfDecisions(i, j, k )

    variable i; variable j; variable k
    string word = "hello"

    if (i == 0)
        print "i == 0"
    else
        print "i != 0"
    endif

    if ( (i == 0) && (j == 1) || (k < 0) )          //more complex condition
        print "complex conditions fulfilled"
    endif

    if (j == 0)
        print "j == 0"
    elseif ( i == 1)
        print "i == 1"
    elseif (k == 2)
        print "k == 2"
    else
        print "j != 0, i !=1 and k !=2 "
    endif

    if ( stringmatch(word,"hello") )          //short for if (stringmatch(..)!=0)
        print "Word is 'hello'"
    else
        print "Word is not 'hello'"
    endif

    //if can also work with numbers only
    if(0)
        print "never happens"
    endif
```

```
if(1)
    print "happens"
endif

if(-37.5)
    print "happens as well"
endif

end
```

The if-statement only tests if the numeric value in the bracket is different from zero. Only if it is zero, the else-branch is considered. Accordingly, every function or operation which returns a numeric value can be inserted into the brackets.

Why *elseif*: Both code examples in the following table work as expected, but the one with elseif is shorter and easier to understand at first sight.

if-endif in "else-branch"	Using elseif

if (j<=2)
    print "here"
else
    if (j>=3)
        print "there"
    else
        print "neither here nor there"
    endif
endif
	if (j<=2)
	    print "here"
	elseif (j>=3)
	    print "there"
	else
	    print "neither here nor there"
	endif

switch-case and strswitch-case

switch-case decision structures and their counterparts for string variables, *strswitch-case* structures, are an alternative to if-structures. They test if the content of a variable or string matches a certain case from a limited set of options. If so, the code in the corresponding case segment will be executed. Each case segment needs to close with a break statement. If the break statement is omitted, also the following case segments will be executed! This may or may not be desirable behavior – it is in any way a possible source for unexpected code behavior.

The next function is also part of the module ControlFlow. This time, the string is an optional parameter.

4.5 Flow control in functions

```
static function CaseDecisions(a,[word])

    variable a
    string word

    if (paramIsDefault(word))
        word = "hello"
    endif

    switch(a)
        case 1:
            print "a = 1"
            break
        case 5:
            print "a = 5"
            break
        default:
            print "a is neither 1 or 5"
    endswitch

    // this happens if the break statements are omitted:
    // a very interesting behavior!

    print "omitted break statements"
    switch(a)
        case 1:
            print "a = 1"
        case 2:
            print "a = 2"
        case 3:
            print "a = 3"
        case 4:
            print "a = 4"
        case 5:
            print "a = 5"
        default:
            print "a is a number greater than", a-1
    endswitch

    // strings have a special switch-structure
    strswitch(word)
        case "hello":
            print "word = hello"
            break
        case "world":
            print "word = world"
            break
```

47

```
        default:
            print "word = ", word
    endswitch

end
```

4.5.2   Loops

Igor offers two types of loops:

1. for-loop
2. do-while-loop

for-loop

The *for-loop* is rather straightforward, as shown by the next example (in the module ControlFlow). The expression within the parentheses is composed of three individual expressions: (<starting instruction for the loop>; <condition to stay in the loop>; <instruction at the end of each iteration>). The condition will be checked before each iteration.

```
static function ForLoop()

    variable i

    print "Ascending for loop "
    for (i=0; i<10; i+= 1)
        print i
    endfor

    print "Descending for loop"
    for (i=10; i>0; i -= 1)
        print i
    endfor
    print "Completed"

end
```

The for-loop continues as long as the condition is true, that is, different from zero. Therefore, you can construct infinite loops by the statements:

```
//Creates an infinite loop
for (i=0; 1; i++)   //because the condition is always true, i.e., different from 0
    print i
endfor
```

4.5 Flow control in functions

```
for (i=0; -37.5; i++)   //same as above
    print i
endfor
```

Infinite loops can be interrupted by the user with the "Abort Button", which appears during program execution in the bottom right corner of the Igor Pro main window.

The fact that the for-loop continues as long as the condition is different from zero can be used in connection with strings and the function char2num() in an interesting way (see also page 33). In the function below, the loop is only continued as long as char2num() returns values different from zero. The example is also part of the module ControlFlow:

```
static function StringTerm()

    variable i
    string test="Hello World"

    for (i=0; char2num(test[i]) ; i += 1)
        print test[i], char2num(test[i])
    endfor
end
```

do-while-loop
The *do-while-loop* behaves slightly different than the for-loop: the statements are executed at least once. This is because the condition is checked after each iteration, not before (as in the for loop). The next example illustrates how to use the do-while-loop:

```
static function DoLoop()

    variable i=20

    //the loop is entered - but left as soon as
    //the condition is checked
    do
        print i
        i--          // i -= 1 or i = i -1
    while(i<10)

    i=0
    do
        i++          // i += 1 or i = i +1
```

```
    print i
while(i<10)
    print "Completed"
```

end

Infinite loops can be easily constructed with the do-while statement, either by having a constant true condition, or by by-passing the condition statement with a *continue* instruction. The following lines demonstrate these possibilities:

```
do
    //...code
while(1)

//--- alternative way of making an infinite loop --
do
    //...code
    if (1)
        continue
    endif
while(0)   //usually, the do-loop would terminate after the first run
```

break and continue

The last example already demonstrated the effect of the *continue* instruction: it causes a premature jump back to the starting point of a loop. In contrast, the *break* command causes a jump out of the loop. Usually, both commands are only triggered if a certain condition is fulfilled; the next function demonstrates how to use them.

```
static function FlowBreakDemo()

    variable i

    for (i=0; i<10; i+=1)
        print i
        if (i>5)
            continue //premature restart
        endif
        print "Second part of for loop reached"
    endfor

    print "Entering do loop with i = ", i
    do
        i -= 1
        print i
```

```
        if (i<5)
            break
        endif

    while (i>0)

end
```

Use the debugger to follow the program execution line by line. This can be quite instructive.

Summary

In this chapter, you have learned a lot about Igor functions: their internal data-objects, how information is passed between functions, and how to control the program flow within a function. Many of these concepts are not only applicable in Igor, but also in other programming languages; a thorough understanding of these concepts will be a big advantage if you ever decide to learn another programming language.

5 Global Data-Objects in Igor Experiments

5.1 Global data-objects

You can think of an Igor experiment file as an environment for data-objects, and of Igor as the framework that provides methods to deal with them. The data-objects in Igor experiments are:

1. Waves
2. Global variables and global strings
3. Constants and string-constants
4. Data folders
5. Dependencies (formulas)
6. Structure variable definitions
7. Function definitions
8. Paths

The first three items in this list carry values, either numbers or characters. *Data folders* serve as containers for waves, variables, and strings. *Constants* (or *string-constants*) are numeric values (or character sequences) that are defined for the entire Igor experiment and can be used by every function within the Igor experiment. *Dependencies* connect global variables and numeric waves. *Structure variable definitions* provide blueprints for customized data types. *Function definitions* are also global objects – they permanently exist independently of other functions. *Paths* carry information about where an Igor program can read/write information on the hard drive.

All of these objects are usually created by the user, either by importing (experimental) data, or by operations in the Igor file. When creating one of these objects, you have to be aware of some limitations concerning the names of these objects:

1. Names must start with a letter.
2. Names must not be longer than 31 characters (bytes) in Igor 7 and 255 characters (bytes) in Igor 8.
3. If special characters (like "_", ".") are used in the name, you have to enclose the name in single quotation marks (see Igor manual: "liberal names").

5.2 Data-objects for storing numbers and characters

These data-objects are:

1. Waves
2. Global variables and global strings
3. Constants and string-constants
4. Data folders (indirectly – they store waves, variables, and strings)

5.2.1 Waves

Waves are the most important data-objects in Igor. A wave is simply an array (you could also say a list) with individual cells for data, either numeric values, date-and-time entries, strings, or references to other waves. Waves can be up to four-dimensional; in this case, you need four indices to uniquely identify an item of the wave (think of an address consisting of four items: "country", "city", "street", and "house number"). You can access individual cells of a wave with their index (or indices for multidimensional waves) in brackets.

Meta-information carried by waves

Apart from storing numbers, characters, dates/times, and references, waves can also carry meta-information about their contents. We will discuss this for one-dimensional numeric waves. For this case, the meta-information consists of:

- data units
- x scaling and units

By default, the contents of the wave are just plain numbers. You can change this by assigning a *data unit*, e.g., meter or seconds, to these values.
The *x scaling* allows to assign an x-value to every cell of the wave. This makes plotting much easier, since the wave "brings its own x-axis" – in a manner of speaking. It is also possible to assign a physical unit to these x-values.

The following module shows how to create and reference a wave, as well as how to handle scaling and units in waves.

```
#pragma moduleName = WaveScaleDemo

static function main()

    make /N=30 /O root:testWave    // absolute path in experiment file
    wave tW=root:testWave
```

5.2 Data-objects for storing numbers and characters

```
// assign meta-information

SetScale d, -inf, inf,"meter", tw      // assign unit to data values in wave     1)
SetScale /I x, 0, 10,"sec.", tW        // specify x-axis range und unit          2)

//assign values
tW = exp(-x) + enoise(0.05)            // random number with enoise()
display /K=1 tw                         // /K=1: allow closing without asking
print "General information: ", WaveInfo(tw,0)

//Read out scaling information
print "Scaling information of the 1D wave"

print numpnts(tw)         // how many numbers in wave
print deltax(tw)
print leftx(tw)           // the x value of point 0 (first cell of the wave)
print rightx(tw)          // this is NOT the x value of the last point in tw!
                          // see help on rightx()!
print pnt2x(tw,29)        // which x value is at point 29 (last cell of the wave)
print x2pnt(tw,10)        // which point has the x value of 10?

// the following functions are also applicable to waves with more dimensions
print "Scaling information with more general functions"

print DimSize(tw,0)
print DimDelta(tw,0)
print DimOffset(tw,0)
// no counterpart for rightx()
print IndexToScale(tw,29,0)
print ScaleToIndex(tw,10,0)

end
```

If you want to remove the unit from the meta-information, and keep the scaling intact, simply insert the next command into the function.

```
SetScale /I x, leftx(tw), pnt2x(tw,numpnts(tw)-1),"", tW
```

Using rightx(tw) in this command would actually change the scaling! Try this for yourself.

Arbitrary meta-information can be attached to the wave as a string with the operation note and accessed with the function note().
In the data-browser, check the "Info" checkbox in order to access the information associated with waves.

5.2 Data-objects for storing numbers and characters

> 1) The specifier d of the SetScale command allows to assign a unit to the wave's contents. In the example, the unit is "meter". The additional numbers -inf (-infinity) and inf (infinity) give the possible range for numbers in the wave. These numbers are not used by Igor – they are more or less only for your information.
>
> 2) SetScale /I x, 0, 10 specifies the x-interval: The first cell of the wave has an x-value of 0 and the last cell has an x-value of 10. The unit of these x-values is "seconds". As an alternative to the lower and upper values for the interval, you could also use the lower value and the step-width (*delta x*) in connection with the /P flag. SetScale operations with multidimensional waves are demonstrated in the example on page 95.

Specification of cell contents (type and accuracy)

Type and accuracy of the cell contents of waves are primarily set with the flags of the make command. The following module illustrates the different possibilities:

```
#pragma moduleName = WaveDemo

static function main()

    variable i
    //use relative paths: waves are created in currently active data folder

    //-- integer waves

    make /W /N=1000 /O IntegerWave
    wave IW = IntegerWave
    IW = pi

    make /B /N=1000 /O EightBitWave
    wave EBW = EightBitWave
    EBW = pi

    make /I /N=1000 /O ThirtyTwoBitWave
    wave TTBW = ThirtyTwoBitWave
    TTBW = pi

    make /L /N=1000 /O SixtyFourBitWave
    wave SFBW = SixtyFourBitWave
    SFBW = pi

    //-- floating point waves
```

```
//-- single precision is the default precision without any flags
make /N=1000 /O StandardSinglePrec
wave SP = StandardSinglePrec
SP = pi

make /C /N=1000 /O ComplexWave
wave /C CW = ComplexWave
CW = cmplx(pi,2)

// -- double precision, most accurate

make /D /N=1000 /O DoubleWave
wave DW = DoubleWave
DW = pi

make /FREE /D /N=1000 /O FreeDoubleWave
wave DWF = FreeDoubleWave
DWF = pi

//-- other types

make /T /N=100 /O TextWave
wave /T TW = TextWave
TW[0] = num2str(pi)              //limited accuracy!

make /WAVE /O ReferenceWave
wave /WAVE RefW = ReferenceWave
RefW[0]=DW                       //write a wave reference to another wave

make/D/N=10/O dateWave
wave dateW = dateWave
for (i=0; i<numpnts(dateW); i +=1)    //cycle through cells
    dateW[i] = date2secs(2018,4,i)    //note: day 0 of April is 3/31/2018
endfor
SetScale d 0, 0, "dat", dateW    //tell Igor this wave stores date/time data
                                 //by writing "dat" for the unit!
end
```

It is instructive to inspect the resulting waves in the data browser! The number of significant digits that are displayed in a table can be changed via the menu bar: *Table>Modify Columns*. Compare the values in the double and single precision waves to the value of pi from Igor's *arbitrary precision math* methods (APMath /v a=pi on the command line).

The flag /FREE of the make operation creates a wave that behaves like a local object: it disappears once the function, in which it was created, terminates. Such *free waves* cannot be found in the data browser. You can use free waves as local *arrays* (for variables or strings) inside a function.

Multidimensional waves
Waves can have up to four dimensions. Igor refers to these dimensions as "row", "column", "layer", and "chunk". The scaling operations on waves with more dimensions require also additional specifiers (names) for each dimension. In the one-dimensional case, the specifier is x (SetScale /I x ....). For the second, third, and fourth dimension the specifiers are y, z, and t, respectively. An example is given in chapter 8.1.

A two-dimensional wave can be used to represent a mathematical matrix. Igor does, in fact, offer various operations specifically for matrices, e.g., calculation of *eigenvalues*. Multidimensional waves can also be used to store miscellaneous information, for example, color information for font and background of a list box control element.

The next function illustrates how to approach multidimensional waves; it is also part of the module WaveDemo:

```
static function Matrix()

    make /D /N=(3,3) /O MatrixWave
    wave MW = MatrixWave
    MW = 1                       // initialize explicitly
    MW[0][0]=2
    MW[1][1]=3
    MW[2][2]=1
    MatrixEigenV MatrixWave   //demonstrate matrix methods
    //result are written to automatically generated wave

end
```

It is possible to assemble a wave of higher dimensionality from waves of lower dimensionality. In this context, we will use a special syntax with the letters p, q, r, and s, which serves to identify the cell index. The next function from the module WaveDemo demonstrates this.

```
static function assembleHD()

    make/O/N=(10,10,2) targetWave
    wave tG = targetWave
```

5.2 Data-objects for storing numbers and characters

```
tG = 0
make/O/N=(10,10) source1
wave s1 = source1
s1 = pi

make/O/N=(10,10) source2
wave s2 = source2
s2 = pi^2

tG[][][0] = s1[p][q]      //first layer filled with 2D wave s1       1)
tG[][][1] = s2[p][q]      //second layer filled with 2D wave s2

end
```

1) The statement tG[][][0] = s1[p][q] is actually a shortcut for the following construction:

```
variable i,j
for (i=0; i<10; i+=1 )
    for (j=0; j<10; j +=1)

        tg[i][j][0] = s1[i][j]

    endfor
endfor
```

It is also very instructive (!) to observe what happens when tG[][][0] = s1[p][q] is replaced by tG[][][0] = p*q.

You should know… You can inspect multidimensional waves in the data browser. If you open a new table for one of the multidimensional waves (right-click + "Edit"), you can use these buttons on the table window to cycle through the different layers of the wave:

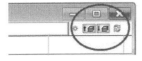

5.2 Data-objects for storing numbers and characters

Here is another example for the application of p, q, r, and s (on the command line, where you do not need a reference). Again, use the buttons in the table window to browse through different dimensions of the wave.

```
make /O /N=(10,10,10,10) BigWave
BigWave =p*q*r*s
print BigWave[2][3][4][5]
BigWave =sin(p)*cos(q)*exp(r)*ln(s)
print BigWave[2][3][4][5]
```

Such shortcuts work also with one-dimensional waves. The dateWave in the module WaveDemo#main() on page 56 could have been initialized with such a shortcut instead of the for-loop:

```
dateW = date2secs(2018,4,p)     //alternative code for WaveDemo#main()
```

Working with waves

There are many Igor commands that work with waves, the most important are listed in the table below. Use Igor's help menu to find more details about these commands.

Duplicate	Duplicate a given wave
Rename	Give a wave a new name
KillWaves	Delete one or more waves
Redimension	Change the dimensions of a wave
Sort	Sort the wave according to a certain criterion
Concatenate	Concatenates two individual waves
WaveExists	Checks if a specified wave exists
note	Append a note with meta-information to the wave; see also note().

Using dimension labels

It is possible to use aliases to access individual cells or groups of cells in a wave. These aliases are called *dimension labels*. Dimension labels can be very useful in connection with multidimensional waves. The following examples work with three-dimensional waves. Again, the module is WaveDemo.

```
static function DimLbl()

    make /O/N=(4,4,3) root:Block
    wave Block=root:Block
```

5.2 Data-objects for storing numbers and characters

```
    //give a label to every layer
    //SetDimLabel 1, ... would work on columns, SetDimLabel 0, .... on rows
    SetDimLabel 2,0,sheet1, Block
    SetDimLabel 2,1,sheet2, Block
    SetDimLabel 2,2,sheet3, Block

    //make a stack: access all cells that belong to a certain layer at once
    Block[][][%sheet1] = 10    //identical to Block[][][0] = 10
    Block[][][%sheet2] = 20    //identical to Block[][][1] = 20
    Block[][][%sheet3] = 30    //identical to Block[][][2] = 30

end
```

Go to the data browser, right-click on the wave "Block", and click "Edit". Again, use the two arrow buttons in the top-right corner of the table window to cycle through the layers.

The following function shows how to use dimension labels to access individual cells in a wave:

```
static function DimLblCellAccess()

    make /O/N=(3,3,3) /T root:Cube
    wave /T Cube=root:Cube

    //give a label to every row
    SetDimLabel 0,0,row0, Cube
    SetDimLabel 0,1,row1, Cube
    SetDimLabel 0,2,row2, Cube

    //give a label to every column
    SetDimLabel 1,0,col0, Cube
    SetDimLabel 1,1,col1, Cube
    SetDimLabel 1,2,col2, Cube

    //give a label to every layer
    SetDimLabel 2,0,lay0, Cube
    SetDimLabel 2,1,lay1, Cube
    SetDimLabel 2,2,lay2, Cube

    //use shortcut to write the indices to the cells
    Cube = "p=" + num2str(p)+" q=" + num2str(q)+" r=" + num2str(r)

    //access the elements via the labels
    print Cube[%row0][%col1][%lay2]
end
```

The "make /O memory effect"

A wave should always be initialized with well defined values to avoid errors – here we will see why. Go back to the matrix example on page 57 and follow the steps below:

1. Modify the code: delete MW = 1
2. Execute the function: WaveDemo#Matrix()
3. Execute: edit MatrixWave
4. Write an arbitrary number into each cell
5. Execute the function WaveDemo#Matrix() again and observe what happens to the matrix

Only the entries along the diagonal have changed back after step 5! The rest of the wave remembered what you did in step 4! Clearly, /O did not really overwrite the old wave (as one could expect).

Similar unexpected effects can happen, if you try to change a wave directly with values derived from itself, without using temporary variables as buffer. Execute DisplayHelpTopic "Don't Use the Destination Wave as a Source Wave" and DisplayHelpTopic "Example: Normalizing Waves" to learn about the details.

5.2.2 Global variables and global strings

A global variable or global string can be created on the command line by executing:

```
variable /G testVar
testVar =2
```

or

```
string /G testWord
testWord = "hello"
```

Upon execution of these commands, both data-objects are visible in the data browser (if the corresponding check-boxes of the data browser are activated). If you want to access the string or variable from a function, you need to create a local reference. This is done by using the keywords NVAR and SVAR for variables and strings, respectively. This has already been demonstrated in chapter 4.

5.2.3 Constants and string-constants

Constants and string-constants cannot be defined via the command line, but only from a procedure file. Constants and string-constants can be defined as static, so they are valid only in the procedure file in which they are defined.

```
#pragma moduleName = AccessConst

static constant ConstA= 3.14
static constant /C ZConst = (2,3)        //complex constant
static strconstant StConst = "hello"

static function main()

    print ConstA
    print real(ZConst), imag(Zconst)
    print StConst

end
```

The constants are strictly encapsulated in the module. The instruction:

```
AccessConst#ConstA
```

does not work! The only way to access these encapsulated constants is via a function in the module.

5.2.4 Data folders

As already mentioned above, you can think of an Igor experiment as a "box" that contains permanent data-objects, namely, waves, global variables, and global strings. The contents of the "box" are visible in the root data folder in the data browser.[13] It can be helpful to create subfolders (smaller "boxes" inside the large "box") within the root data folder. The active (sub)folder of an experiment can be set manually by shifting the red arrow in the data browser.
In a program, data folders can be used for the following purposes:

1. To provide a container for the global variables, strings, and waves which are used during the runtime of a graphical user interface.
2. To store the waves that result from a calculation.
3. To provide a room for backup data.

---

[13] It is possible to transfer individual data-objects from one Igor experiment to another with the "Browse Expt..." button in the data browser.

5.2 Data-objects for storing numbers and characters

On the command line, a new data folder can be created by:

NewDataFolder subFold

The new folder is a subfolder in the current data folder (which is oftentimes the root folder of the experiment). If you want to create a sub-subfolder, you have to mark the current data folder and the hierarchy with ":".

NewDataFolder :subFold:testFold

If a function is supposed to work with a specific global data-object in a specific subfolder, it has to know the *absolute path* to this data-object in the folder hierarchy. In the next command, a global variable is declared and initialized with such an absolute path:

Variable /G root:subFold:testFold:testVar = 1

There are several methods and functions used in connection with data folders[14], but not all of them are equally important. For example: GetDataFolder and GetDataFolderDFR basically serve the same purpose. However, GetDataFolder is somewhat outdated and its use is not recommended any longer.

Some important methods which are used in connection with data folders and programming are:

- pwd, GetDataFolder, GetDataFolderDFR
- cd, SetDataFolder
- NewDataFolder
- dir, DataFolderDir
- DataFolderExists
- DuplicateDataFolder
- KillDataFolder
- RenameDataFolder
- MoveDataFolder

If you want to work with data folders in a program, you can use local references, using the keyword "DFREF". The following program illustrates this concept.

---

[14] See also the Igor help file "Data Folders.ihf"

```
#pragma moduleName=Datafolders

static function main()

    make /D /O /N=100 yWave     //create a wave in the currently active data folder
    wave yW = yWave             //make a reference
    SetScale /I x 0,2, yW
    yW = x^3

    NewDataFolder /O root:Calculations     // create a data folder
    DFREF dfr = root:Calculations          //make a reference

    // copy the wave into the folder and display it
    duplicate /O yW, dfr:yWaveCopy         // try also: MoveWave
    display dfr:yWaveCopy

end
```

Note the frequent use of the /O flag to force overwriting and prevent errors.[15] The similarity between the ways in which waves and data folders are treated is apparent here: first creation, then referencing, followed by usage.

Chapter 8 contains several examples that demonstrate how data folders can be used in a program. Going further into details is at this point not fruitful – Igor's help files are quite clear on data folders and programming with data folders. Before leaving this topic, it should be mentioned that it is also possible to generate *free data folders*, like it is possible to generate *free waves* (page 57).

5.3   Data-objects that store meta-information

The data-objects that we will discuss now do not carry alphanumeric values. Instead, they provide information *about relations* between waves and variables (dependencies), *locations* on the hard drive (paths), or provide blueprints for customized data types (structure variables) and methods (functions).

---

[15] You have to keep in mind that the overwrite flag with waves does not protect from errors due to memory effects. See page 61.

5.3.1 Dependencies

A *dependency* is a data-object that links a global variable to a numeric wave. A synonym for dependency is *formula*. The dependencies in an experiment can be viewed via *Misc>Object Status*. It is easy to define a dependency with the ":=" operator. Here is how it is done on the command line[16]:

```
variable /G freq=2
make /D /N=1000 /O DependentWave
SetScale /I x, -pi,pi, DependentWave
DependentWave := cos(freq*x)
```

Now, whenever you change the global variable "freq" (either manually in the data browser, on the command line, or with a function), the values in the wave are automatically updated. This becomes apparent by executing:

```
Display DependentWave
freq=8
```

The operator ":=" cannot be used in a user-defined function, instead you have to use the command SetFormula. The Igor manual cautions against using too many formulas.

5.3.2 Structure variable definitions

Structure variable definitions have already been covered in chapter 4.2.4. They are mentioned here again only for completeness. Such definitions are global elements, which can be accessed by various functions. However, structure variables are local data-objects. Examples are given on pages 95, 118, and 126.

5.3.3 Function definitions

From a certain perspective, function definitions are a sort of global object, too. They exist permanently and can be used in different functions. Consequently, Igor offers the possibility to generate references to functions by using the keyword FUNCREF. This is an advanced programming technique, which allows telling a function dynamically which other function to call. Using function references can be useful, but it necessarily involves at least one non-static function. So, this usefulness comes with a price: the danger of creating name conflicts between functions. An example is given on page 127.

---

[16] On the command line, no wave reference is needed.

5.3.4 Paths

Paths are used in the context of file operations on the hard drive. If you want to open a specific file on the hard drive with a program, you need to create a symbolic path with the command `NewPath`. Paths are not visible in the data browser. Instead, they can be managed via the menu bar:

- *Misc>New Path...*
- *Misc>Path Status...*
- *Misc>Kill Path...*

Chapter 7.2 demonstrates the practical application of paths during reading and writing operations on the hard drive.

6 Strings, Characters, and Output

6.1 Fundamental properties of strings

Strings carry character sequences (words) and are very useful data-objects. For this reason, Igor offers a large number of functions to work with strings. According to the Igor manual, strings can contain approximately two billion characters (bytes) and can also contain lists of character sequences. They are initialized with their contents inside quotation marks.

1. Regular strings
   `string word = "Apple"`

2. List strings: different items, usually separated by ";"
   `string manyWords = "Apple;Orange;Cherry"`

3. Key-value lists: lists that contain "key:value" combinations as items
   `string dict = "Fruit1:Apple;Fruit2:Orange;Fruit3:Cherry"`

Lists can be very useful to store information. The list separator (usually ";") can be customized in list strings and key-value lists.
The key-value list is known as "dictionary" in Python; generally, such data types are known as "mappings".

It is important to remember that list-strings are a special class of strings and key-value lists are a special type of lists. That means that you can use all string methods with a list-string and all list-string methods with a key-value list. The reverse is not true: you cannot use a method which is specific for list-strings with a regular string.

Strings are useful in many situations:

- Together with the operator "$", you can use them to create dynamic references to objects.
- Many Igor functions return list-strings or key-list-strings that contain, for example, lists of all waves in a certain data folder or lists with all curves on a given graph.
- Inside a function, you can use them in a similar manner as arrays, i.e., you can save a given set of numbers or characters inside a string.
- It is also possible to store text-description patterns in a string. Such text-description patterns are known as regular expressions (see chapter 6.6).

6.2 Handling individual ASCII/Unicode characters

Text encoding changed drastically from Igor Pro 6.x to Igor Pro 7. This chapter will deal exclusively with the situation in Igor Pro 7.x and higher versions.

Generally, a computer does not know letters or symbols, but only numbers in its memory; a certain number in the computer's memory is associated with a certain character. The most fundamental rule to associate a number with a character is given by the *American Standard Code for Information Interchange* (ASCII). This code associates the numbers 0 to 127 with letters and symbols.

However, a modern computer needs more than just 128 characters. Therefore, the ASCII table was several times augmented by further number-character association rules that provide a far greater repertoire of characters. One of these augmentations is Unicode (UTF-8, UTF-16).

The numbers which are used to identify characters are usually given in the decimal or hexadecimal system. In Igor, the functions num2char() and char2num() allow to translate between number and character.

The *hexadecimal* numbers that represent a certain character can be stored in a string by using specific *escape sequences*. A \u or \x escape sequence at the beginning of a string tells Igor to interpret the string as a Unicode character and treat the number (which follows the escape sequence) as the hexadecimal identification number for a certain character. Note that there is a difference between lower-case and upper-case u in the escape sequence: \u does have a different meaning than \U. According to the manual, \U represents rare Unicode characters.

The following examples illustrate these concepts (for details about printf see page 76). Try them on the command line.

```
//prints a capital A using 41(hex)=65(dec)=101(oct)
print U+0041
print "\x41"            // \x is two-digit(!hex)code UTF-8
print "\u0041"          // \u four digit hex code UTF-16
print "\101"            // \ddd is interpreted as octal number
printf "%c\r",65
print num2char(65)

//print a small Greek lambda
//there is no two-digit hex code for this character
print U+03BB
print "\u03BB"
print "\xCE\xBB"        //four digit hex code
printf "%c\r",995       //does not work like the others, printf expects ASCII
print num2char(955)

//print the yen symbol
print "\xC2\xA5"
print "\u00A5"
```

The Unicode hex numbers are not arbitrarily chosen for Igor, but follow the Unicode standard. You can find them easily online.

6.3 Operations with strings

The definition of a string is done with the assignment operator "=" and double quotation marks " ". Strings can be connected with the concatenation operators "+" and "+=".

```
string word = "hello" + " world!"
```

Accessing string elements can be done elementwise with the character index in brackets [ ].

```
print word[4]
```

It is possible to *insert* (not substitute!) further characters elementwise with the character index in brackets [ ].

   word[4]="OOO"; print word

The operator "[ ]" can also be used to access various elements at once:

   print word[2,4]

And it destroys multiple-byte characters:

   word ="\u03BB "; print word
   word[1]="A"; print word

The table below gives a summary of other string methods in Igor. Two of them, SplitString and GrepString, work with *regular expressions* (chapter 6.6). Most of these methods have more (optional) parameters. However, these details can be easily looked up in the command help. The examples in the table are chosen so that the basic behavior of the methods gets clear.

Task	Command	Example
Measure length	Strlen	print strlen("hello")
Compare two strings	StringMatch[17] CmpStr	print StringMatch("hello","world") print StringMatch("hello","*lo") print CmpStr("B","A")
Split up string (according to a known regular expression)	*SplitString*	string source = "20,oranges" string expr="([[:digit:]]+),([[:alpha:]]+)" string part1, part2 SplitString /E=(expr) source, part1, part2 print part1 print part2

---

[17] StringMatch does accept the wildcard character * to stand for an arbitrary number of any character. "!" at the beginning is interpreted as NOT. The wildcard feature can cause unexpected behavior for dynamic (user-entered) strings. Note the "inverse" return values (to identical strings) of CmpStr and StringMatch.

Remove characters at start and end	TrimString RemoveEnding	print TrimString(" abc ") print RemoveEnding("dataset1.txt",".txt")
Substitute characters	LowerStr UpperStr, ReplaceString	print LowerStr("aBc") print UpperStr("aBc") print ReplaceString("b", "abcb", "B") print ReplaceString("bc", "abcb", "BC")
Search contents	StringSearch *GrepString*	print StrSearch("abcde", "cde",0) print GrepString("hallo","[0-9]") print GrepString("hallo","[a-z]")
Append and remove trailing characters	PadString UnPadString	string test ="hello" string padded = PadString(test,20,0x21) print padded string unpadded = UnPadString(test,0x21) print unpadded

Conversion of strings:

Conversion functions allow to convert data-objects of one type into another. They can be used to generate, e.g., the number 3.14 from the string "3.14" and vice versa. Here is a list with the conversion functions for strings:

str2num(), num2str(), num2istr(), char2num(), num2char()

The functions num2char() and char2num() are interesting on a very fundamental level. The regular way of initializing a string works with the characters on the keyboard. However, you can also use the Unicode numbers as an alternative. In the following example, both strings contain the word "hello".

```
string regInitString = "hello"
string ASCIIinitString = num2char(104)
ASCIIinitString += num2char(101)
ASCIIinitString += num2char(108)
ASCIIinitString += num2char(108)
ASCIIinitString += num2char(111)
print ASCIIinitString, regInitString
```

In most cases, it is by far too complicated to initialize a string with the Unicode characters. However, if you wish to use characters that are not available on a standard keyboard, this way of doing it can be useful. If you need to get the Unicode number of a certain symbol (e.g., for elementwise comparison of the characters in a string), you can use the function char2num(). This function expects a one-character string as parameter (therefore, you have to use quotation marks together with the character).

The conversion functions num2str(), num2istr(), and str2num() allow a conversion between numeric variables and strings. They offer only a limited accuracy, as already demonstrated on page 32.

6.3.1 Analyzing strings with sscanf

The function sscanf allows extracting information from a string. It was apparently designed to be close to its counterpart in C. The basic syntax of sscanf is as follows:

    sscanf <scanned string>, <pattern string>, <variable to take scan result>

The pattern string is a formal description of the string which is scanned: it shows the sscanf command where to find the values that should be extracted. Here is an example:

```
#pragma moduleName = sscanfDemo

static function main()

    variable val1, val2
    string ScannedString = "x-Value: 1, yValue: 2"
    string PatternString = "x-Value: %d, yValue: %d"
    sscanf ScannedString, PatternString, val1, val2
    print val1, val2

end
```

The string which describes the pattern is a perfect copy of the scanned string, with one exception: the parts of the string which should be extracted to variables are specified with a %d. Here, %d causes sscanf to interpret the extracted values as decimal integer values.

There are several other specifiers apart from %d. For the conversion of string contents to integer variables, the specifier %i is the most flexible. It can actually distinguish between octal, decimal, and hexadecimal numbers. If the number in the string is in the regular format ("1234"), it is interpreted by %i as decimal. If it starts with a zero ("01234"), it is interpreted as octal number. If it starts with 0x ("0x1234"), it is interpreted as hexadecimal integer number. In all cases, it is saved to a numeric variable in its decimal representation!

Alternatively, you can interpret simple integer numbers as octal or hexadecimal numbers by using the %o or %x specifier, respectively.

You can further specify a decimal integer variable as strictly positive (unsigned) by using %u. But: if the scanned string should contain a negative number at a spot which is specified as %u, an error will result. The same is true for %x and %o.

Of course, sscanf is not restricted to integer values. The specifier %e marks a floating point real number. Interestingly, the specifiers %f and %g serve exactly the same purpose – which introduces a certain degree of redundancy at this point.

It is also possible to extract substrings by using the specifier %s.

So far, the pattern string had to be a nearly perfect copy of the scanned string – the only difference which was allowed was that the characters of interest in the scanned string had been substituted with specifiers in the pattern string.

But what if you do not know about the exact form of the scanned string in advance? In this case, sscanf can be used more flexible with character classes (this is somewhat similar, but not(!) identical, to the character classes in regular expressions), using the specifier %[ ]. The next function, also from the module sscanfDemo, illustrates this:

```
static function CharClasses()

    variable val1, val2
    string word1, word2
    string ScannedString = "x-Value: 1, yValue: 2"
    string PatternString = "%[a-zA-Z-]: %d, %[a-zA-Z]: %d"
    sscanf ScannedString, PatternString, word1, val1, word2, val2
    print word1, val1
    print word2, val2

end
```

The word "x-Value" is described with the pattern: *{one or more letters between a and z} + {one or more letters between A and Z} + hyphen at some location.* The word "yValue" is described by the same pattern without the hyphen. However, many more words are described by the same patterns, thus sscanf is much more flexible now. Still, if you remove the last hyphen from the first character class, making it %[a-zA-Z], sscanf fails because "x-Value" consists of more than just letters.

sscanf can also be used in user-defined functions which read files from the hard drive.

6.3.2 Changing string contents with sprintf

The command sprintf does the opposite of the command sscanf. It allows to insert information into a string. The syntax of sprintf is similar to the command printf, but with an additional specification of the target string. See chapter 6.5 on page 76 on formatted printing for more details. The following code inserts a number into a string at the location given by the location of the specifier %e.

    sprintf TargetString, "contents that go to the Target: %e", 3.1415

The specifiers for sprintf are similar, but not identical, to the specifiers for sscanf.

6.3.3 Escape sequences in strings

Strings may not only contain regular keyboard characters, but also further (non-printing) characters like tabulator steps or line breaks. These non-printing characters are referred to as *escape sequences* and are marked in the string by a backslash \.

Escape sequences can also be used for individual characters to mark them as hexadecimal or octal representations of, e.g., a Unicode symbol. In the following command (enter on the command line), Unicode escape sequences are used to print characters which are not usually part of a keyboard layout.

    print "\u2154\u2022\u0128\u2360"

There are several other *escape sequences* in addition to \u, all marked by a backslash. The most important ones are \r (return carriage), \n (newline), and \t (tabulator step). print "\nHello\tWorld" starts a new line and also prints a tabulator step between "Hello" and "World".

Further information about escape sequences is available in the Igor Pro manual, chapter IV-1, "Escape Sequences in Strings".

6.4 List strings and key-value lists

List strings are strings in which individual words are separated by a special character (unless specified otherwise by a semicolon ";"). An example for a list string is: "apple;orange;cherry".

A key-value list is a list string in which each item follows a "keyword:value" pattern. An example for a key-value list is:
"fruit1:apple;fruit2:orange;fruit3:cherry".

Always remember that list strings and key-value lists must not contain whitespaces! The index of the individual items in the list starts at zero!

6.4.1 List strings

List-strings feature additional methods, and many Igor methods return lists of (data-)objects.

List-strings are a subclass of strings and all string methods can be used with them. The table below summarizes the functions which are *additionally* available for list strings. There, GrepList is the only function which uses *regular expressions* (page 78). Most of the functions below actually have several optional parameters, which can easily be found in the Igor's command help. The examples are selected so that the behavior and intention of the functions gets clear.

Task	Command	Example
Get number of items	ItemsInList	print ItemsInList("a;b;c")
Read items	StringFromList	print StringFromList(2, "a;b;c")
Add items	AddListItem	print AddListItem("d","a;b;c") print AddListItem("d","a;b;c",",") print AddListItem("d","a;b;c",";",3)
Remove items	RemoveListItem RemoveFromList	print RemoveListItem(2,"a;b;c;d") print RemoveFromList("a","a;b;c;a")
Sort through list	SortList	print SortList("c;d;a;b;1;2;18") print SortList("c;d;a;b;1;2;18",";",16)
Analyze	WhichListItem FindListItem *GrepList* ListMatch[18]	print WhichListItem("ac","aa;ab;ac") print FindListItem("ad","aa;ab;ac;ad") print GrepList("aa;ac;a1;b2","[[:digit:]]") print ListMatch("aa;ab;ac","*b")

---

[18] Like StringMatch, ListMatch accepts the wildcard character * to stand for an arbitrary number of any character. "!" at the beginning is interpreted as NOT.

6.4 List strings and key-value lists

Conversions:
wfprintf, ListToTextWave, ListToWaveRefWave, WaveRefWaveToList

The conversion routines for lists are designed in a way that the individual entries of a list can easily be converted to the individual entries of a wave and vice versa.

wfprintf can (despite its actual purpose of writing wave contents to files) write the contents of a text-wave to a string:

```
#pragma moduleName = FormattedPrint

function WaveCont2String()

    make /O /T /N=3 TextWave
    wave /T tw = TextWave
    tw[0]="Apple"; tw[1]="Cherry";tw[2]="Orange"

    string list = " "

    wfprintf list, "%s;", tw
    print list

end
```

Built-in operations that produce lists with Igor (data-)objects:
For completeness, several important operations that return lists are compiled below:
StringList, VariableList, WaveList, WinList, TraceNameList, SpecialCharacterList, PictList, PathList, OperationList, MacroList, IndependentModuleList, ImageNameList, GuideNameList, FontList, CTabList, ControlNameList, ContourNameList, ChildWindowList, AxisList, AnnotationList

6.4.2 Key-value lists

Key-value lists are identical to list-strings, with one special requirement: the list items are "key:value" combinations. For these special types of lists, a few further specialized methods exist. Key-value lists are a subgroup of list strings. Therefore, one can use all methods from lists, for instance to add new key-value pairs.

Task	Command	Example
Get contents	StringByKey NumberByKey	print StringByKey("a1","a1:A;b2:B;c3:C") print NumberByKey("a1","a1:1;b2:2;c3:3")
Substitute/ Add	ReplaceStringByKey ReplaceNumberByKey	print ReplaceStringByKey("a1","a1:A;b2:B","Z") print ReplaceNumberByKey("a1","a1:1;b2:2",9)
Remove	RemoveByKey	print RemoveByKey("c3","a1:A;b2:B;c3:C")

6.5 Formatted printing

Formatted printing means generating output with additional information or with the application of certain rules. Igor offers four commands for this purpose: printf, fprintf, wfprintf, and sprintf standing for "print formatted", "file print formatted", "wave file print formatted", and "string print formatted", respectively.

6.5.1 Formatted printing to the command line: printf

The instruction how to format the output is encoded with a "%", followed by a specifier character which is either e, E, f, g, G, d, u, b, o, x, X, s, c, or W – in total 14 choices. Out of these 14 choices, only two, s and c, do not work with numbers. W allows introducing units into the output – the command help for printf describes how to use this specifier. In general, it is fair to say that $\mathtt{printf}$ is mainly a method to bring numbers into a nice output format. Accordingly, printf allows to display decimal numbers in different styles, depending on the specifier:

```
printf "%e\r", 31415920000
printf "%f\r", 31415920000
printf "%g\r", 31415920000
```

With the specifier %d, printf can be used to round a decimal value (round "away from zero") to an integer.

```
printf "%d\r", 9.2
```

printf can be used to get number representations of a decimal number in the binary, octal, and hexadecimal representation by using the specifiers %b, %o, and %x, respectively. You can quickly try these examples on the command line.

6.5 Formatted printing

```
printf "%b\r", 13
printf "%o\r", 9
printf "%x\r", 8
```

The following table summarizes the effects of the specifiers for the number 42.5:

e	4.250000e+01	d	43	X	2B
E	4.250000E+01	u	43	s	invalid
f	42.500000	b	101011	c	*
g	42.5	o	53		
G	42.5	x	2b		

Additional formatting instructions can be inserted between the % and the specifier character with flag characters. These are:

- \-   align left in the field
- +   always write a "-" or "+" in front of the number
- <space> insert some space before a positive number
- #   apply individual special rules when e, f, g, or x are used as specifiers

Furthermore, it is possible to control the precision with which a number is displayed (printed) by printf. Writing a decimal point followed by a number supplies this information: .4 gives the instruction to have 4 digits after the decimal separator.

In addition, you can control the total number of digits (field width) by using a second number before the decimal separator. The instruction 10.4 will create a field of ten digits – four of them after the decimal separator.

The specifier character is also a description of the variable which is subject to printf. Therefore, the combination %u (unsigned) and negative numbers do not give a valid answer.

Chapter 8.9 on page 112 contains a program with which it is possible to visualize the effects of different printf formatting instructions on arbitrary numbers. This tool can be used to visualize instructions like: %+012.3f, %-4.2g, or %#10.7e.

6.5.2 Formatted printing into strings and files

The operations sprintf, fprintf, and wfprintf follow the same syntax:

command <destination>, <pattern string>, <source>

Each of these three functions has a specific source and target data-object.

Source	Destination	Method	Discussion/example
variable / string	string	sprintf	page 73
variable / string	file	fprintf	page 87
wave	file / string	wfprintf	page 75

6.6 Regular expressions

Regular expressions are widely used in many modern programming languages, and this chapters is supposed to give you a glimpse into their application in Igor Pro.

Regular expressions are a systematic way to describe *text patterns*; thus, they are usually applied to strings. A simple analogy to a regular expression is "*.txt", where * stands for any character or set of characters. Application of this pattern, e.g., in the search dialog of a file browser, will result in a list with all files that have the suffix ".txt"; the file browser interpreted the "*.txt" as an instruction to look for a pattern. Igor is capable of similar things, but the syntax is different and a little bit more complex than in the introductory example ("*" and "." have a specific meaning in Igor).

In order to work with regular expressions, a programming language needs functions which are aware of the meaning of regular expressions. There are several string functions in Igor which fulfill this condition:

- GrepString
- SplitString
- GrepList
- Grep (does not work directly with strings)

In general, there is usually more than one way to construct a regular expression to describe a given string. On the other hand, there is usually more than one string matching a given regular expression.

Implementation in Igor

In order to define text patterns, a set of rules and characters is required. The full list of special characters that are used to define regular expressions is:

- { } matched exactly {n} times
- [ ] allows to specify a set of characters: character class
- ( ) grouping and scope
- ^ defines a prefix; logical NOT in a character class [^
- $ defines a suffix
- . matches any single character (POSIX)
- | boolean OR
- * zero or more occurrences of the preceding element
- ? zero or one occurrences of the preceding element
- + one or more occurrences of the preceding element
- - defines a range, e.g., [0-9]
- : used in the definition of a POSIX character class, e.g., [:ascii:]

The text-description patterns that are built with these characters are also saved inside a string.

If you want to include these characters in the text pattern as well, you have to mark them with a backslash. For example: ? is interpreted as the "zero-or-one occurences" quantifier, but \? is interpreted as question mark.

There is a peculiarity about the backslash in Igor: Igor strings can include escape characters which are marked as such by a backslash. If a backslash is actually part of pattern, it is not sufficient to write "\\" but you have to double one of them: "\\\".[19] This behavior is somewhat counterintuitive.

Here is a small code segment that illustrates the basic usage of regular expressions:

```
string test = "2+2=4"
print GrepString(test,"2\+2")  //prints 1 because 2+2 is in the string

test = "C:\WIN32"
// a string like this one can only be created manually in the code
// - Igor cannot display this correctly!
```

---

[19] Igor tries to avoid single backslashes in a string. If a backslash is entered into a string, e.g., via a set variable GUI control element, Igor will double the backslash. For example: if the user enters C:\Win32, Igor will save C:\\Win32 automatically. This feature is somewhat hidden and can cause confusion.

```
// if you enter a single \  (e.g., via a 'set variable' control element)
// Igor will save it as \\

print GrepString(test,"C:\\\WIN") //prints 1
test = "housekeeper"
print GrepString(test,"keeper")    //prints 1
print GrepString(test,"^(house)")  //prints 1
print GrepString(test,"^(keeper)$") //prints 0
print GrepString(test,"(keeper)$") //prints 1
```

Character classes

Character classes are defined by using [ ]. When working with character classes, you have to remember a few basic properties:

Character class	Meaning
[abc]	a OR b OR c
[(ab)c]	a OR b OR c: the parentheses () have no effect
abc	a AND b AND c
[^abc]	not a OR not b OR not C
[ab[:^alpha:]]	a OR b OR any non-letter

Practicing regular expressions

Regular expressions are usually not complicated, but you have to practice how to read them correctly – in the opinion of the author there is no way around this simple fact.

The following list gives several additional examples. However, no list can actually cover all possible expressions.

Meaning	regular expression
One or more letters (case sensitive) between a and z	[a-z]
bat, cat, rat **but not** at	[bcr]at
bat, rat, hat **but not** cat or at	[^c]at
Waldo, undone **but not** distro	do
do, door, doomed **but not** undone	^(do)
review, preview **but not** reviews	(view)$
boat or cat	((bo)|c)at

6.6 Regular expressions

The program "RXCheck" (see page 115) allows to write, test, and understand any regular expression. You should use this little tool to achieve mastery of regular expressions; after all, they are a general and important concept in programming, not only in Igor Pro, but also Python, Java, Perl, PhP, and many other programming languages. And they can be a fun puzzle, too.

Part III

Special Topics and Examples

In order to write robust and usable programs, a programmer sometimes needs subtle and hidden details. Oftentimes, just seeing "how it's done" is enough to induce a steep increase in the learning curve.

7 Special Topics

7.1 Bit parameters and bit operators

Bit parameters

The idea is basically very simple: Suppose a function is controlled with a binary number, e.g., 000101. Then, the function learns what to do by analyzing on which positions the binary number contains a 1. If a single 0 or 1 digit is called a bit, then the function learns what to do by analyzing which bit is set (to 1). In the table below, the binary number has seven bits, the index starts at zero.

Binary number to control function behavior	Index of the bit which is set (to 1)	Number represented in hexadecimal system	Number represented in decimal system
0000001	0	(0x01)	1
0000010	1	(0x02)	2
0000100	2	(0x04)	4
0001000	3	(0x08)	8
0010000	4	(0x10)	16
0100000	5	(0x20)	32
1000000	6	(0x40)	64

7.1 Bit parameters and bit operators

Several functions expect parameters where a "bit is set". Unfortunately, you cannot(!) just write a statement like variable controlV=0000001. Instead, Igor expects either the index at which the bit is set to 1, or the hexadecimal (or decimal) representation of the control variable. Thus, by supplying a statement like variable controlV=0x40 (decimal representation: 64) you can set bit number 6 ($2^6 = 64$). This approach is somewhat counterintuitive but not complicated.

Appendix C shows how the behavior of a list box element (for graphical user interfaces) is controlled by bit parameters.

Bit operators

In the case above, numbers, and, more specifically, their (internal) binary representations were used as control variables. The binary representations of numbers can be used further by *bitwise operators*. The concept of bitwise operations is also know in other programming languages. They are based on the logical OR and AND operations which are given by the following table:

Value 1	Value 2	Logical AND	Logical OR
0	0	0	0
0	1	0	1
1	0	0	1
1	1	1	1

Given two binary numbers with n digits, you can compare these numbers with the logical AND and OR *bitwise*. That means that bit n of number 1 is logically compared with bit n of number 2 – and this is repeated for all bits. The next table illustrates this idea.

0001 1000 bitwise AND *0000 result*	0001 1111 bitwise AND *0001 result*	0110 1001 bitwise AND *0000 result*
0001 1000 bitwise OR *1001 result*	0001 1111 bitwise OR *1111 result*	0110 1001 bitwise OR *1111 result*

Of course it is somewhat clumsy to work with binary numbers. Therefore, Igor's bit operators work with the decimal representations of the binary numbers instead. The operators are "&" for the bitwise AND and "|" for the bitwise OR. The examples in the last column of the table connect 0110 (decimal 6) and 1001 (decimal 9). In the first case (AND) the result is 0000 (decimal 0). In the second case (OR) it is 1111 (decimal 15). The "&" and "|" operators reproduce these results on the command line:

print 6 & 9   result 0

print 6 | 9   result 15

Here is the full list of binary operators:

- & bitwise AND
- | bitwise OR (inclusive)
- %^ bitwise OR (exclusive)
- ~ bitwise complement: make a 0 to 1 and vice versa
  printf "%b\r", 7; printf "%b\r", ~7
  In connection with &, it can be used for clearing certain bits:
  set bit 3 ($2^3=8_{dec}=1000_{bin}$) from the number $12_{dec} = 1100_{bin}$ from one to zero. Afterwards, $4_{dec} = 0100_{bin}$ is left over.
  printf "Binary:%b\r", 12&~8; printf "\rDecimal: %d\r", 12&~8
- \>\> bitshift to the right
  print 8 >> 1   results in 4
  because 2^3 is shifted to 2^2, or in binary: 01000 is shifted to 00100
- << bitshift to the left
  print 8 << 1   results in 16
  because 2^3 is shifted to 2^4, or in binary: 01000 is shifted to 10000

Note that the bitshift operators shift the entire binary number. In the case of >> this can lead to a loss of the original zero-bit: 0101 shifted by one bit to the right gives 0010.

7.2 Accessing the hard drive

Igor does not only allow to access data-objects within an Igor experiment – it also allows to read files from the hard drive and write files there as well. Igor's programming language is, in this respect, similar to any other programming language, in particular C. Igor can also deal with folders on the computer's hard drive.

7.2.1 Reading and writing files

The first example shows the simplest possible approach to open, read, and close an ASCII text file. Before you run this program, create a plain text file with the following entries (separated by a tab-step):

File: test.txt

1	1
2	4
3	9
4	16

Save it to a suitable location on your hard drive where you have writing permission. Then, create a new module named "fileOps", enter and execute the following Igor code. When the program is started, an open file dialog appears. Navigate to the location where the file test.txt is saved and click "Open".

```
#pragma moduleName = fileOps

static function MiniLoad()

    variable refIn
    string buffer
    variable xval, yval

    Open/R /Z=2 refIn          //open file, /Z=2 for opening the dialog

    if (V_Flag)                //user canceled dialog.
        return 1               //V_Flag is created implictly by Open!
    endif

    do                         //loop through the lines
        FReadLine refIn, buffer

        if (strlen(buffer) == 0)
            break              //end of file reached, exit now
```

```
        endif

        sscanf buffer, "%g\t%g", xval, yval
        print xval, yval
    while(1)

    Close refIn              //close file

end
```

Only three commands are needed: Open, FReadLine, and Close. The file is identified with a reference number (variable refIn) and not with its path or a string variable. The flag /R indicates that the file is opened in reading mode.

The program above shows the simplest approach. However, Igor offers many more commands to facilitate the work with ASCII and binary files.

- Open
- FReadLine
- sscanf (to deal with the individual lines)
- Close
- MoveFile (also for renaming)
- DeleteFile
- fprintf
- wfprintf ("wave file print formatted")
- FStatus
- FGetPos
- FSetPos
- FBinWrite (for binary files)
- FBinRead (for binary files)

Working with paths and writing files

The program example above receives the file path by calling an open file dialog. This behavior can be avoided by setting the file's location on the hard drive already in the program. To do so, add two lines of code and change the open command:

```
string fileName ="test.txt"
NewPath /O FileDir "C:Users:Admin:Desktop"    //depends on your system

//open the file
Open /R /P=FileDir refIn as fileName
```

NewPath /O generates a path with which Igor can work: this is called a *symbolic path*. The flag /O overwrites any existing path with the same name. It is

7.2 Accessing the hard drive

instructive to omit the /O flag and see what happens when the program is called repeatedly. The command Open has many options – and can be quite useful. Consult the command help to get more information.

Apart from reading files, Igor is also capable of writing files to the hard drive. This is not very complicated. The writing is achieved by the function fprintf ("file-print-formatted") – the procedure is straightforward.

In the next example, Igor will be used to copy an ASCII file. Add the following code to the module "fileOps":

```
static function CopyFiles()

    variable refIn, refOut
    variable xval, yval
    string buffer

    string fileIn ="test.txt"
    string fileOut ="testCopy.txt"

    NewPath /O OriginalDir "C:Users:Admin:Desktop"
    NewPath /O CopyDir "C:Users:Admin:Desktop"
    //use a location to which you have writing permission

    Open /R /P=OriginalDir refIn as fileIn
    Open /P=CopyDir refOut as fileOut

    do
        FReadLine refIn, buffer

        if (strlen(buffer) == 0)
            break           // end of file
        endif

        sscanf buffer, "%g\t%g", xval, yval
        fprintf refOut, "%g \t %g\r\n",xval, yval

        //failsafe line-breaks: \r\n
        //although \r is enough for most text editors
    while(1)

    Close refIn
    Close refOut

end
```

87

Further functions which are useful in this context are:

- IndexedFile
- IndexedDir
- ParseFilePath

7.2.2 Creating folders on the hard drive

Folders on the hard drive are created with the command NewPath and the flag /C. This is somewhat counterintuitive, but you can see it as creating a folder together with the path. The following command creates an additional folder on the author's desktop together with the path variable myPath. Try it on the command line after adapting the path to your system.

    NewPath /O /C myPath "C:Users:Admin:Desktop:NewFolder"

There are several methods available to work with folders:

- MoveFolder
- CopyFolder
- DeleteFolder
- SetFileFolderInfo
- GetFileFolderInfo

7.3 Creating a help file

When a program is distributed, it can be helpful to provide new users with additional information about the program. The most convenient way to achieve this is by writing one or more help files.

The way by which you can create an Igor Pro help file is explained in great detail in the manual in volume IV. The following instructions provide, in a nutshell, the required steps. For any more in-depth information consult the Igor manual.

Igor help files are compiled during startup, so a certain syntax has to be followed. You can create a help file from scratch with a formatted notebook:

1. Open a new formatted notebook window (*Windows>New>Notebook* and activate the "Formatted Text" check box). Select a suitable name.

2. At the top of the help file, you need to define a "ruler" which is called "Topic". To do so, follow these instructions:

7.3 Creating a help file

   a. At the top left corner of the formatted notebook window is a drop-down menu. The current item is "Normal".
   b. Select the drop-down menu and click on "Define New Ruler ...".
   c. In the dialog enter "Topic" as new ruler name, then click OK.

3. The topic of the help file has to be *marked with a bullet point* character, *followed by a tabulator step*, and *then the keyword* under which the help file should be found later on in Igor's help. Proceed as follows:

   a. Use a Unicode expression to copy a bullet character "•" to the clipboard: execute `PutScrapText U+2022` on the command line.[20]
   Alternatively, use the mouse and Ctrl/Cmd+C to copy a bullet point from Igor's history area, or use *Edit>Special Characters...*
   b. Paste it with Ctrl/Cmd+V to the formatted notebook into the section marked as "Topic" at the very beginning of the document.
   c. Add a tabulator step right after the bullet character.
   d. Add the topic name (= *keyword*) right after the tabulator step.
   e. Press Enter on your keyboard.
   f. Once the cursor is in the next line, select "Normal" from the drop-down menu in the top left corner.

4. Start to enter the contents of the help file.

5. When finished with editing, save the formatted notebook as Igor help file with the suffix .ihf into the "Igor Help Files"[21] folder. Use *File>Save Notebook As...*

6. Restart Igor, the help file will be compiled during start up.

---

[20] The hexadezimal code expression U+2022 for the bullet point can be found online when doing a quick web search for "unicode bullet point".

[21] This folder is (like "User Procedures" and "Igor Procedures") in the "Igor Pro User Files" folder.

89

7. Now the help file is available via *Help>Help Topics* where you can find it under its file name.

If you want to edit an existing help file, follow the steps below. Make sure that the file browser of your operating system does not hide the file type!

1. Use your file browser to go to the folder in which the help file is stored. Igor must be closed
2. Change the suffix of the help file from .ihf to .ifn
3. Double click on the .ifn file – Igor starts up
4. Do the editing, save the edited .ifn file with *File>Save Notebook*
5. Close Igor
6. Go back to the folder with the help files and change the suffix back to .ihf
7. Open the help file with a double click and check if everything is like you wanted it

7.4 Handling errors during runtime

The try-catch-endtry statement allows Igor to continue executing a program – despite a runtime error. The following module demonstrates this:

```
#pragma ModuleName = ErrorDemo

static function BasicRTE()

    wave w=NonExistent          //this will cause an error

    try                         //if an abort happens, go to the catch sequence
        Display w; AbortOnRTE   //if there is a runtime error: do the abort
    catch
        variable err = GetRTError(1)  //clear the error
    endtry

    print "Going on"

end
```

In this example, the abort command is triggered when a runtime error occurs with the Display command. However, this is not a "true" abort, as the program is merely redirected to the catch statement, where the error is cleared. From there on, the program continues until the end of the function is reached.

Alternatively to "waiting" for a runtime error, the program code can also be redirected to the catch segment if a variable takes a certain value. This can be achieved by the command AbortOnValue. AbortOnValue is, in contrast to AbortOnRTE, called with two parameters: the abort condition and the numeric abort code which should be associated with this specific abort.

AbortOnRTE or AbortOnValue generate an implicit variable called V_abortCode. The abort code from the AbortOnValue statement is written to this variable. AbortOnRTE sets V_abortCode to -4 by default. Further options are listed in the Igor manual.

Here is a prototypical example for AbortOnValue:

```
static function AbOnVal(a,b)

    variable a,b

    //these variables are indicators for the type of error

    variable DivisionByZero = 1
    variable DivisionByNaN = 2      //NaN = not any number
    variable DivisionBy42 = 3       //suppose we do not want to devide by 42

    try
        AbortOnValue b==0, DivisionByZero
        AbortOnValue numtype(b)==2, DivisionByNaN
        AbortOnValue b==42, DivisionBy42

        //only if all three tests b==0, numtype(b)==0, and b==42 were negative
        //the following code is executed. == does not work with NaN!

        print "ratio =", a/b
    catch
        variable err = GetRTError(1)           //clear the error
        print "The error code is: ", V_AbortCode   //V_AbortCode is implicitly created
    endtry

end
```

After the error has been cleared, and the commands within the catch-section have been executed, the program proceeds normally until the end of the function.

7.5 The conditional operator "?:"

This operator provides a shortcut for an if-decision and behaves in a certain aspect like a function: it returns a well-defined numeric value.

The following code illustrates the behavior:

```
#pragma moduleName = CondOp

static function getAbsolute(val)

    variable val
    variable result

    print "Enter a positive or negative number"

    result = ( val >= 0 ? val : val*(-1) )
    print "Result: ", result

end
```

If the number supplied by the user is positive, its value will be assigned to the output variable named "result". If the number is negative, its value multiplied by -1 will be assigned to the output variable.

The next function has a focus on the condition:

```
static function Decision(trigger)

    variable trigger
    variable result

    result = ( trigger ? 10 : -10 )
    print "Result: ", result

end
```

Observe the results for CondOp#Decision(-3), CondOp#Decision(324), and CondOp#Decision(0).

The conditional operator does not(!) work with strings! In this case, SelectString() could be an alternative.

7.6 What else is out there?

The purpose of this book is not to provide an exhaustive discussion of all features available to the Igor programmer. However, it cannot harm to give a few pointers to what is possible:

- Use cursors and marquees as input devices
- Read and write binary files
- Do image processing
- Do matrix operations and higher math
- Control a webcam to create a live-feed into Igor
- Make contact to the www with Igor's ftp methods
- Use Igor for data acquisition
- Write Igor extensions with other programming languages
- Work with sounds
- Read out screen resolution and adapt graphical user interfaces accordingly
- Conditional compilation
- Hard-coding images (ASCII85 format) into panel definitions

In the author's experience, the following check list turned out to be very helpful during program development:

1. Do I precisely know what I want?
2. What are the global data-objects in my program? Which data-objects exist before program execution? Which data-objects are created by the program?
3. Where in the root folder are these objects? Where do I want to have them?
4. Do I explicitly reference all of them?
5. Are implicit compiler actions (like implicit references) or similar shortcuts avoided, and if not, do I have a good reason not to avoid them?
6. Do I understand what I can do with the data-objects that I use? Am I using Igor's help menu in the best possible way?
7. Is the program encapsulated in a module? If not, do I have a good reason to keep it not encapsulated?
8. Is there a smarter and clearer way?

8 Sample Programs

This chapter contains the following examples:

1. A simple example for structures
2. Storing parameters in strings vs. waves
3. Calculating curves #1
4. Calculating curves #2
5. Finding the location of a wave on a graph
6. Normalizing curves in a plot
7. Making an .avi animation
8. A simple genetic algorithm
9. A tool to observe the output of printf (GUI)
10. A tool to check regular expressions (GUI)
11. An interactive function plotter (GUI)
12. A calculator frontend (GUI)
13. Remote control of Igor with batch files – and remote control of the operating system with Igor via batch files
14. An example with a hook function (GUI)
15. An example with function references
16. A simple neural network for curve fitting

All programs in this chapter follow the module-static approach. This avoids name conflicts and allows encapsulating the code as far as possible.

Some programs also feature concepts that have not been covered in the main text, for instance, the use of cursors as input devices, or the use of graphs within panels as subwindows. Interesting code segments are highlighted in bold font.

The paths in some of the programs in this chapter are set to folder names on the author's computer. You will have to adapt these paths to your system.

Sample Programs

8.1 A simple example for structures

Idea:
Using structures is a simple way to avoid global variables or passing long argument lists to functions. Although they are described in the Igor manual as advanced feature, their application is actually straightforward. Structure variables are local data-objects and they cannot be used to save information permanently.

Usage:
Execute the function from the command line.

Comments:
You can also write functions to deal with a specific type of structure. In the code below, the function "ParameterSet_GiveAverage(s)" is specifically made to work with a structure of type "ParameterSet". Not every function that receives a structure must be that specific; consider, for example, a function which only prints the name of the structure, or something similar unspecific.

Code:

```
#pragma moduleName = StructApp

//----
//-- define a new type of data-object 'ParameterSet'
//-- and some functions to work with this data type
//----

static Structure ParameterSet
    variable var1
    variable var2[2]   // array - an unusual construction in Igor
                       // limited to a length of 100
endStructure


static function InitializeParameterSet(s,n)

    struct ParameterSet &s
    variable n
    s.var1= 2^n
    s.var2[0]= pi/2
    s.var2[1]= 4

end
```

95

Sample Programs

```
static function ParameterSet_GiveAverage(s)

    struct ParameterSet &s
    variable average = 0
    average = 1/3 * (s.var1 + s.var2[0] + s.var2[1])
    return average

end


//----
//-- this is the module's main routine
//----

static function main()

    struct ParameterSet Set1
    InitializeParameterSet(Set1,1)

    struct ParameterSet Set2
    InitializeParameterSet(Set2,2)

    make /D /N=(100,100,100,100) /O MultiDim
    wave MDW = MultiDim
    SetScale /I x, -5, 5, MDW
    SetScale /I y, -5, 5, MDW
    SetScale /I z, -5, 5, MDW
    SetScale /I t, -5, 5, MDW

    // make a wave which depends on the structure's members
    MDW = Set1.var1*x + Set1.var2[0]*y + Set1.var2[1]*z + sqrt(abs(t)+5)

    // do some evaluation
    print "First average: ", ParameterSet_GiveAverage (Set1)
    print "Second average: ", ParameterSet_GiveAverage (Set2)

end
```

Sample Programs

8.2 Storing parameters in strings vs. waves: runtime comparison

Idea:

During function execution, the (transient) parameters can be stored in waves or strings. Which version is faster? (On the author's computer, the differences in runtime between Igor 7 and Igor 8 were significant, with Igor 8 being much faster.)

Usage:

Call the function from the command line.

Code:

```
#pragma moduleName = SpeedComp

static function main()

    variable i, result, timerRefNum
    variable timeString = 0
    variable timeWave = 0

    // measure the time associated with the string
    result = 0
    timerRefNum = startMSTimer                      //microsecond timer
    string parameterList = "2,-1,3,5,10,9,12"

    for ( i = 0; i < 7; i += 1)
        result += str2num( StringFromList( i, parameterList, ",") )
    endfor

    timeString = stopMSTimer(timerRefNum)
    print "String: ",timeString

    // measure the time associated with the wave
    result = 0

    timerRefNum = startMSTimer

    // use a free wave, so it does not survive as a global object
    make /FREE /D /N=7 parameterWave
    wave paraWavePointer = parameterWave

    paraWavePointer[0] = 2
    paraWavePointer[1] = -1
    paraWavePointer[2] = 3
    paraWavePointer[3] = 5
```

Sample Programs

```
    paraWavePointer[4] = 10
    paraWavePointer[5] = 9
    paraWavePointer[6] = 12

    for ( i = 0; i < 7; i += 1)
        result +=paraWavePointer[i]
    endfor
    timeWave = stopMSTimer(timerRefNum)

    print "Wave: ", timeWave
    print "Ratio string/wave: ", timeString/timeWave

end
```

Sample Programs

8.3 Calculating curves #1

Idea:

Use Igor to calculate functions and store the values in waves. Use Igor as a graphical calculator.

Usage:

Call the function from the command line.

Code:

```
#pragma moduleName = MakeCurves1

static function main()

    variable i

    make /D /N=1000 /O Simulation
    wave sim = Simulation
    SetScale /I x, -5, 20, sim

    sim = exp( - 0.25*( x - 2 )^2 ) * sin( 2* ( x-1.9) )

    // make a copy of the wave and give it a reference
    duplicate /O sim SimulationB
    wave simB = SimulationB
    SimB = 0

    make /D /N=(10,2) /O coefficientWave        // make a 2D wave
    wave coefPointer = coefficientWave

    for ( i = 0; i < 10; i += 1 )
      // create a random number between -2 and 2 and save it
      coefPointer[i][0] = 2 * enoise(1)

      // create a random number between -5 and 20 and save
      coefPointer[i][1] = 25* ( 0.5 + enoise(0.5)) - 5

      // add a gaussian peak, the coefficients
      // are taken from the wave 'coefficientWave'
      SimB += coefPointer[i][0] * exp( - ( x - coefPointer[i][1] )^2 )

    endfor

end
```

8.4 Calculating curves #2

Idea:
As the previous example, but now the parameters are stored in different types of lists.

Usage:
Execute the function from the command line.

Code

```
#pragma moduleName = MakeCurves2

static function main()

    make /D /N=1000 /O Simulation2
    wave sim2 = Simulation2
    SetScale /I x, -5, 5, sim2

    duplicate /O sim2 SimulationC
    duplicate /O sim2 SimulationD
    duplicate /O sim2 SimulationE
    wave simC = SimulationC
    wave simD = SimulationD
    wave simE = SimulationE

    // string access by index

    string parameterList = "237"
    sim2 = str2num( parameterList[0] )
    sim2 += str2num( parameterList[1] ) * x
    sim2 += str2num( parameterList[2] ) * x^2

    // list access by stringFromList

    string parameterList2 = "-1, -2, -3"
    simC = str2num( StringFromList( 0, parameterList2, ",") )
    simC += str2num( StringFromList( 1, parameterList2, ",") ) *x
    simC += str2num( StringFromList( 2, parameterList2, ",") )  * x^2

    // NO WHITESPACES in those key lists

    string parameterList3 = "para1:-1;para2:5;para3:-8"
    simD = str2num(  StringByKey("para1", parameterList3) )
    simD += str2num(  StringByKey("para2", parameterList3) ) *x
    simD += str2num(  StringByKey("para3", parameterList3) )  * x^2
```

Sample Programs

```
    string parameterList4 = "para1: -2;para2:3;para3:-10"
    simE = NumberByKey("para1", parameterList4)
    simE += NumberByKey("para2", parameterList4)  *x
    simE += NumberByKey("para3", parameterList4)  * x^2

end
```

Sample Programs

8.5 Finding the location of a wave on a graph

Idea:

1. The user creates a plot with one or more spectra.
2. Later on, the user has many plots and waves in the experiment; all waves are located in different subfolders within the experiment.
3. The user picks a graph and wants to know the specific location of a wave on that graph in the experiment.
4. The wave of interest is marked with a cursor. After the user calls the function, the absolute path to the wave is printed to the command line.

Usage:

1. Select a graph
2. Mark the wave of interest with a cursor (Ctrl/Cmd+I and mouse)
3. Go to the command line and type LocateWave#main()

Code:

```
#pragma moduleName=LocateWave

static function main()

    strswitch ( CsrWave(A) )

        case "":     //A is not on the graph
            strswitch (CsrWave(B))
                    case "":      // B is not there either
                        DoAlert 0, "You have to use the cursors"
                        return 1
                    default:      // B is there
                        wave BPointer = CsrWaveRef(B)
                        print "Cursor B is on: "
                        print GetWavesDataFolder(BPointer,2)
                        break
            endswitch
            break

        default:    // A is on the graph

            strswitch (CsrWave(B))
                    case "":    //B not
                        wave APointer = CsrWaveRef(A)
                        print "Cursor A is on: "
                        print GetWavesDataFolder(APointer,2)
                        break
```

Sample Programs

```
            default:  // A and B are both on the graph
                      wave BPointer = CsrWaveRef(B)
                      print "Cursor B is on: "
                      print GetWavesDataFolder(BPointer,2)
                      print "Cursor A is on: "
                      wave APointer = CsrWaveRef(A)
                      print GetWavesDataFolder(APointer,2)
                      break
          endswitch
          break
    endswitch

end
```

8.6 Normalizing spectra/curves in a plot

Idea:
1. First, create a plot with several curves.
2. Normalize every curve on the graph to either:
   - (i) its y value at the left side
   - (ii) its y value at the right side
   - (iii) the difference between the curve maximum and the y value at the left side
   - (iv) the difference between the curve maximum and the y value at the right side

The normalization happens only as **offset** and **muloffset** on the plot; the actual data will remain unchanged. The code should work independently of the current data folder on any plot.

Usage:
1. Pick a graph and make it the top graph by clicking on it.
2. Go to the command line and type DisplayNormalized#main(<specifier>) (where <specifier> stands for a number which determines the modus of normalization).

Sample Programs

Code:

```
#pragma moduleName = DisplayNormalized

static function main(specifier)

    variable specifier
    variable normFac
    variable i

    string CurrentWaveName
    string topGraph = WinList("*", "", "WIN:")
    string ListOfCurves = TraceNameList(topGraph,";",5)
    //setting bit 0 and 2: 101(dual) = 5(decimal)

    variable numberCurves = ItemsInList(ListOfCurves)

    for ( i = 0; i < numberCurves; i += 1)
      CurrentWaveName = StringFromList( i, ListOfCurves)
      wave currentWave = TraceNameToWaveRef( topGraph, CurrentWaveName)

      if (specifier == 0)          //normalize to first point
          normFac =currentWave[0]
          ModifyGraph muloffset($CurrentWaveName)={0,(1/normFac)}

      elseif (specifier == 1)      //normalize to last point
          normFac =currentWave[ numpnts(currentWave) – 1 ]
          ModifyGraph muloffset($CurrentWaveName)={0, (1/normFac) }

      elseif (specifier == 2)      //normalize to difference Max – first point
          normFac  = WaveMax(currentWave)
          normFac -=  currentWave[0]
          ModifyGraph muloffset($CurrentWaveName)={0, (1/normFac) }
          normFac = currentWave[0] * (1/normFac)
          ModifyGraph offset($CurrentWaveName)={0, -normFac }

      elseif (specifier == 3)      //normalize to difference Max – last point
          normFac  = WaveMax(currentWave)
          normFac -=  currentWave[ numpnts(currentWave) – 1 ]
          ModifyGraph muloffset($CurrentWaveName)={0, (1/normFac) }
          normFac = currentWave[numpnts(currentWave) - 1]*(1/normFac)
          ModifyGraph offset($CurrentWaveName)={0, -normFac }
      else
          print "unknown argument, choose an integer between 0 - 3"
      endif
    endfor
end
```

8.7 Making an .avi animation

Idea:

Illustrate how animations can be created. The animation will show a sine-wave and a second wave with a different wave length (due to the Nyquist-criterion).

Usage:

Call it from the command line with AnimateNyquist#main().

Code:

```
#pragma moduleName = AnimateNyquist

static function main()

    variable i
    variable freq = 3.1

    make /O /D /N=20 sampling
    wave sampling = sampling
    SetScale /I x, 0,10, sampling

    make /O /D /N=1000 sineWave
    wave sineWave = sineWave
    SetScale /I x, 0,10, sineWave

    PathInfo SaveDir     //if this path doesn't exist yet,
                         // V_Flag is set to zero
    if (V_Flag == 0)
        //set a folder where you have writing permissions
        NewPath SaveDir "C:Users:Admin:Desktop:"
    endif

    for (i=0; i<35; i += 1)
        sampling = sin(pi*freq*x + 2*pi*0.05*i)
        sineWave = sin(pi*freq*x + 2*pi*0.05*i)
        Display /K=1 /N=nextFrame  sineWave, sampling
        ModifyGraph mode(sampling)=4,marker(sampling)=19
        ModifyGraph rgb(sampling)=(0,0,0)
        ModifyGraph msize(sampling)=7, rgb(sineWave)=(0,34816,52224)
        SetAxis left -1,1

        if (i==0)
            NewMovie /O /P=SaveDir as "Nyquist.avi"
        else
            AddMovieFrame
```

Sample Programs

```
        endif
        DoWindow /K nextFrame
    endfor
    CloseMovie

end
```

Sample Programs

8.8 A simple genetic algorithm to find a word

Idea:

Use a simple genetic algorithm to find a secret word. This program can be used to get a feeling about the effects of population size and mutation probability in genetic optimization. The code should also demonstrate how to work with optional parameters, random numbers (enoise), ASCII encoding, two-dimensional waves, and how to do sorting operations. This example is at an intermediate level of complexity.

Usage:

Try various combinations of mutation rate and population size and see how long it takes until the genetic routine has solved the puzzle. The first argument gives the maximum number of generations after which the program terminates. Compare for example:

FindSecret#main(600)

FindSecret#main(600,mutationProb=0.1,individuals=100)

to explore how a deviation from the standard values changes the ability of the algorithm to solve the puzzle and find the secret word.

Code:

```
#pragma moduleName = FindSecret

//----
//--This function uses some new(!) Igor 7 features!
//--
//--the operator '++'  --->    i++ can be used instead of i+= 1
//--the SortColumns operation ---> sort a multidimensional wave
//--
//--There are other (better) methods for solving the task of
//--getting a 'secret' word. The genetic approach
//--is, however, very instructive from a
//--programmer's point of view. That is why it is done here.

static function main(generations,[mutationProb,individuals])
    variable generations
    variable mutationProb
    variable individuals
```

Sample Programs

```
mutationProb = (ParamIsDefault(mutationProb) ? 0.05 : mutationProb)
individuals = (ParamIsDefault(individuals) ? 1000 : individuals)

string secret = "Santa Claus is coming!"
variable lengthSecret = strlen(secret)
variable i,k,j
variable parentIndex
string gene =""
string parentGenes = ""

// make a two-dimensional text-wave to store the "genepool"
// the first column stores a string with the individual's genes,
// the second column stores the number of correct characters
// "Santa Clerx" "8"
// if the number of correct characters == lengthSecret
// the solution was found!

print "---------------------------------- Starting search!"
print " "

//set up a genepool as a free (transient) 2D-textwave

make /FREE /T /N=(individuals,2) GenePool
wave /T gP = GenePool

//
// make the first generation
//

for (i=0; i<individuals; i++)
    gP[i][0]=""
    gP[i][1]="0"
    for (k=0; k<lengthSecret; k++)

        //get a random number between 30 and 127
        //and interpret it as ASCII code by using num2char
        //(0.5 + enoise(0.5)) generates a random number between 0 and 1
        //use floor for rounding to integer values

        gene = num2char(floor(30+97*(0.5+enoise(0.5))))
        gP[i][0] += gene

        //test if this newest gene is correct, if yes: increase score by one
        if(char2num(gene) == char2num(secret[k]))
            gP[i][1] = num2str( str2num( gP[i][1] ) + 1 )
        endif
    endfor
endfor
```

Sample Programs

SortColumns /A /R /KNDX=1 sortWaves=gP

```
//sort by score, i.e., sort by number of correct characters
//without '/A' 1,13,9 is sorted as 9,13,1
//(sorting by the first character)

//
//now do the further generations
//

for (j=0; j<generations; j++)

    //leave the best 10% of the previous generation untouched
    //start the for loop at a higher i

    for (i=floor(0.1*individuals); i<individuals; i++)
        gP[i][0]=""
        gP[i][1]="0"

        for (k=0; k<lengthSecret; k++)

            //allow a mutation with a certain probability

            if ( (0.5+enoise(0.5)) < mutationProb)
                //draw again a random ASCII character
                gene = num2char(floor(30+97*(0.5+enoise(0.5))))
                gP[i][0] += gene

                if (GrepString(gene,secret[k]))
                    gP[i][1] = num2str( str2num( gP[i][1] ) + 1 )
                endif

            else //no mutation
                //pick a random individual from the best 10%
                parentIndex = floor(0.1*individuals*(0.5+enoise(0.5)))
                parentGenes = gP[parentIndex][0]
                gP[i][0] += parentGenes[k]

                if (char2num(parentGenes[k])==char2num(secret[k]))
                    gP[i][1] = num2str(str2num(gP[i][1])+1)
                endif

            endif //end mutation-choice

        endfor //end loop over individual letters (genes)
    endfor //end loop over individuals (rows in genePool)
```

Sample Programs

```
        SortColumns /A /R /KNDX=1 sortWaves=gP

        print "Generation",j+1,":", gP[0][0]

        if (str2num(gP[0][1])==lengthSecret)
                print " "
                print "Puzzle solved! "
                break
        endif
    endfor  //end loop over further generations

end
```

Sample Programs

8.9 A tool to observe the output of printf

Idea:

Build a graphical user interface to study the effects of different printf instructions. You should define the geometry as demonstrated in chapter 3.

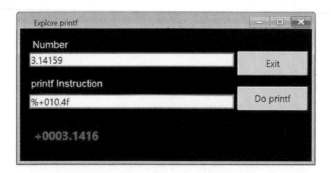

Usage:

Call the program from Igor's menu bar

Code:

```
#pragma moduleName = printfExplore

menu "MyFunctions"
    "Explore printf", printfExplore#call()
    //this is the only part which is not encapsulated
end

static function call()

    //this will write "1" into V_Flag if the window is open already
    DoWindow printfPanel
    if (V_Flag )
            DoWindow /F printfPanel   // if already open, bring to front
            return -1                 // and leave
    endif
    draw()
    init()

end
```

112

Sample Programs

```
static function draw()

    NewPanel /W=(150,77,499.5,232) /K=2 /N=printfPanel as "Explore printf"

    ModifyPanel cbRGB=(0,0,0)
    SetDrawLayer UserBack
    SetDrawEnv textrgb= (65535,65535,65535)
    DrawText 15,26,"Number"
    SetDrawEnv textrgb= (65535,65535,65535)
    DrawText 13,71.5,"printf Instruction"

    Button Check,pos={260.00,67.00},size={85.00,29.00},title="Do printf", fSize=11
    Button Exit,pos={260.00,26.00},size={85.00,29.00},title="Exit", fSize=11

    SetVariable setNumber,pos={11.00,28.50},size={245.00,16.50}, fSize=11
    SetVariable setPrintfInst,pos={11.00,77.00},size={245.00,16.50}, fSize=11
    TitleBox showResult, pos={17.00,115.50}, size={4.00,19.00}, title=" ",fSize=14
    TitleBox showResult, frame=0, fStyle=1

end


static function init()

  NewDataFolder /O root:printfExplore

  variable /G root:printfExplore:Number= 3.141592
  String /G root:printfExplore:pfStr = "%+010.4f"

  SetVariable setPrintfInst,win=printfPanel,value=root:printfExplore:pfStr
  SetVariable setPrintfInst,win=printfPanel,title=" "
  SetVariable setNumber,win=printfPanel,value=root:printfExplore:Number
  SetVariable setNumber,win=printfPanel,title=" "
  SetVariable setNumber,win=printfPanel,limits={-inf,inf,0}

  Button Check,win=printfPanel, proc=printfExplore#ApplyFormat
  Button Exit,win=printfPanel, proc=printfExplore#exit
end


static function ApplyFormat(ctrlName)

  string ctrlName

  NVAR Number = root:printfExplore:Number
  SVAR pfStr = root:printfExplore:pfStr
  string answer = ""
```

Sample Programs

```
    sprintf answer, pfStr, Number
    TitleBox showResult, win=printfPanel, title=answer, fcolor=(0,50000,0)

end

static function exit(ctrlName)

    string ctrlName
    DoWindow /K printfPanel
    KillDataFolder /Z root:printfExplore

end
```

Sample Programs

8.10 A tool to check regular expressions

Idea:

Build a graphical user interface for a simple input and evaluation of regular expressions.

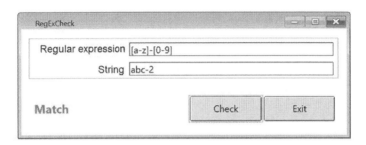

Usage:

Call it from Igor's menu bar

Code:

```
#pragma moduleName = RXCheck

menu "MyFunctions"
    "RegExCheck", RXCheck#call()
        //this is the only part which is not encapsulated
end

static function call()

    //this will write "1" into V_Flag if the window is open already
    DoWindow RegExPanel
    if (V_Flag )
        DoWindow /F RegExPanel    // if it is already open, bring to front
        return -1                 // and leave
    endif

    draw()
    init()

end
```

115

Sample Programs

```
static function draw()

    NewPanel /N=RegExPanel /W=(343,98,734,223) as "RegExCheck"
    ModifyPanel cbRGB=(65534,65534,65534)
    SetDrawLayer UserBack
    DrawText 22,30.5,"Regular expression"
    DrawText 92,55,"String"

    Button Check,pos={203.00,80.00}, size={85.00,29.00},title="Check",fSize=11
    Button Exit,pos={291.00,80.00}, size={85.00,29.00},title="Exit",fSize=11
    SetVariable setRegEx,pos={130.00,16.50}, size={245.00,16.50},fSize=11
    SetVariable setString,pos={130.50,39.50}, size={245.00,16.50},fSize=11

    TitleBox showResult,pos={15.00,84.00}, size={4.00,19.00}, title=" ",fSize=14
    TitleBox showResult,frame=0, fStyle=1

    GroupBox Group pos={9.00,11.50},size={372.00,48.00}

end


static function init()

    NewDataFolder /O root:RegExCheck
    String /G root:RegExCheck:TestString= ""
    String /G root:RegExCheck:RegExString = ""

    SetVariable setString,win=RegExPanel, value=root:RegExCheck:TestString,title=" "
    SetVariable setRegEx,win=RegExPanel,value=root:RegExCheck:RegExString,title=" "

    Button Check,win=RegExPanel, proc=RXCheck#compare
    Button Exit,win=RegExPanel, proc=RXCheck#exit

end
```

Sample Programs

```
static function compare(ctrlName):ButtonControl

    string ctrlName
    SVAR testString = root:RegExCheck:TestString
    SVAR regEx = root:RegExCheck:RegExString
    variable answer = GrepString(testString,regEx)

    if (answer == 1)
        TitleBox showResult, win=RegExPanel, title="Match",fcolor=(0,50000,0)
    else
        TitleBox showResult, win=RegExPanel, title="No match",fcolor=(40000,0,0)
    endif
end


static function exit(ctrlName):ButtonControl

            string ctrlName
            DoWindow /K RegExPanel
            KillDataFolder /Z root:RegExCheck

end
```

8.11 An interactive function plotter

Idea:

Use an embedded graph on a panel to view a function. The function can be manipulated with a slider control element. There are a few special features in the code:
1. It uses the modern and more advanced way of implementing control element functions by using structures.
2. It has the name of the panel hard coded as a string-constant.
3. It demonstrates the application of subwindow statements with the operator "#".

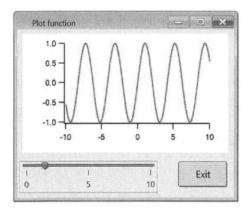

Usage:
Call it from Igor's menu bar.

Code:

```
#pragma moduleName = Plotter

static strConstant panelName = "PlotPanel"

menu "MyFunctions"
  "Function Plotter", Plotter#call()
  //this is the only part which is not encapsulated
end
```

Sample Programs

```
static function call()

    //this will write "1" into V_Flag if the window is open already
    DoWindow $panelName
    if (V_Flag )
        DoWindow /F $PanelName    // if already open, bring to front
        return -1                  // and leave
    endif

    draw()
    init()

end


static function draw()

    NewPanel /W=(150,54,394,244.5)/K=2 /N=$panelName as "Plot function"
    Slider ParaSld,pos={4.00,148.00},size={155.50,32.00}
    Slider ParaSld,limits={0,10,1e-3},value= 0,vert= 0
    Button ExitBtn,pos={184.50,147.00},size={55.00,28.50},title="Exit"
    Display/W=(6,5,240,137)/HOST=#        //setting up a subwindow with #
    RenameWindow #,panelDisplay           //this is all subwindow syntax
    SetActiveSubwindow ##

end


static function init()

    //create the global data-objects associated with the panel
    //use data folder and variable references instead of hard-coded paths

    NewDataFolder /O root:$panelName
    DFREF home = root:$panelName

    variable /G home:para = 0
    NVAR pRef = home:para

    make /D /N=1000 /O home:PlotWave
    wave pWref = home:PlotWave
    SetScale /I x, -10,10,pWref

    Slider ParaSld,win=$panelName,variable=pRef, proc=Plotter#refresh
    Button ExitBtn,win=$panelName,proc=Plotter#exit
    AppendToGraph /W=#panelDisplay pWref   //relative subwindow path

end
```

```
//the button functions are implemented with the help of
//structures - a somewhat more advanced feature
//one has to look up the members of the corresponding structures
//in the Igor manual

static function exit(ButtonProperties)

    struct WMButtonAction &ButtonProperties

    if (ButtonProperties.eventCode == 1)   //mouse down event
        DoWindow /K $panelName
        KillDataFolder root:$panelName
    endif
    return 0

end


static function refresh(SliderProperties)

    struct WMSliderAction &SliderProperties
    //get access to the data-objects
    DFREF home = root:$panelName
    NVAR para = home:para
    wave target = home:PlotWave
    target = sin(para*x)

    return 0

end
```

Sample Programs

8.12 A calculator frontend

Idea:

Build a graphical user interface for input and evaluation of mathematical expressions.

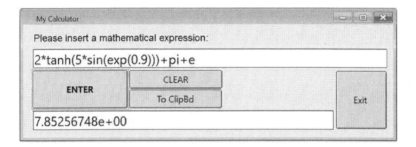

Usage:

Call it from Igor's menu bar

Code:

```
#pragma moduleName = Calculator

menu "MyFunctions"
  "Calculator", Calculator#call()
end


static function call()

	DoWindow CalcPanel          //this will write "1" into
	                            //V_Flag if the window is open already
	if (V_Flag )
		DoWindow /F CalcPanel
		return -1
	endif
	draw()
	init()

end
```

Sample Programs

```
static function draw()

    NewPanel /K=2 /N=CalcPanel /W=(268, 63, 731.5, 201.5)as "My Calculator"
    ModifyPanel cbRGB=(60928,60928,60928)
    SetDrawLayer UserBack

    DrawText 13,24,"Please insert a mathematical expression:"
    Button Enter, pos={12,56.5}, size={119.5,46.5}, title="ENTER", fSize=11,fStyle=1
    Button Clear, pos={134.00,56.50},size={115.00,22.50}, title="CLEAR", fSize=11
    Button ToClipbd, pos={134.00,80.50},size={114.50,22.50}, title="To ClipBd", fSize=11
    Button Exit, pos={392.00,57.50},size={62.50,70.50},  title="Exit ", fSize=11

    SetVariable Input, pos={12.00,30.00},size={444.00,24.00},title=" ",fSize=16
    SetVariable Output, pos={12.00,105.50},size={377.00,24.00},title=" ",fSize=16
    SetVariable Output, valueBackColor=(65535,65535,65535), noedit = 1

end


static function init()

    NewDataFolder /O root:MyCalculator
    string /G root:MyCalculator:CommandString = ""
    string /G root:MyCalculator:resultString = ""
    variable /G root:MyCalculator:result

    Button Enter, win=CalcPanel, proc=Calculator#SendToCommandLine
    Button Clear, win=CalcPanel, proc=Calculator#ClearAll
    Button ToClipbd, win=CalcPanel, proc=Calculator#ToClipBd
    Button Exit, win=CalcPanel, proc=Calculator#ExitMyCalc

    SetVariable Input,value= root:MyCalculator:CommandString
    SetVariable Output,value= root:MyCalculator:resultString

end


static function SendToCommandLine(ctrlName) : ButtonControl

    string ctrlName
    SVAR currentString = root:MyCalculator:CommandString
    SVAR resultString = root:MyCalculator:resultString
    NVAR resultPointer = root:MyCalculator:result
    resultPointer = 0

    //Add the string with the mathematical expression to an instruction
    //which assigns the result to the global variable "result".
    //The full instruction is sent to the command line and executed
```

Sample Programs

```
    string localCommandString = "root:MyCalculator:result = "+currentString
    Execute /Q /Z localCommandString
    // Now, the calculation is done, and the result is saved in the global variable
    sprintf resultString, "%.8e",resultPointer   //make a formatted output
    SetVariable Output,value=resultString

end


static function ClearAll(ctrlName):ButtonControl

    string ctrlName
    SVAR currentCommand = root:MyCalculator:CommandString
    SVAR resultString = root:MyCalculator:resultString
    NVAR resultPointer = root:MyCalculator:result

    currentCommand = ""
    resultPointer = 0
    resultString ="0"

    //clear the content of the clipboard
    PutScrapText ""
    SetVariable Output,value=resultString

end


static function ExitMyCalc(ctrlName):ButtonControl

    string ctrlName
    DoWindow /K CalcPanel
    KillDataFolder /Z root:MyCalculator

end


static function ToClipBd(ctrlName):ButtonControl

    string ctrlName
    NVAR resultPointer = root:MyCalculator:result
    string ClipString

   //copy a formatted output to the clipboard
    sprintf ClipString, "%.8e", resultPointer
    PutScrapText ClipString

end
```

Sample Programs

8.13 Remote control of Igor with batch files – and remote control of the operating system with Igor via batch files

Idea:

This program shows the interplay between Igor and the operating system of the computer. Igor is called from a batch file (assuming that Igor.exe is in the path variable of the operating system) and executes several commands which are saved in an igor-text file (.itx). The commands in the Igor text file actually create a new batch file with additional commands and then execute this new batch file.

The batch file and the .itx file are in the same folder (e.g., the Desktop) on the hard drive! Instructions how to create a batch file can be easily found online.

After the program has completed, there should be a new batch file "OSops.bat" and a new folder "Test" which contains a plot.

Note that all commands within the igor-text file have to start with a capital X.

You need to make a few preparations in order to make the example work:

1. Your operating system must be configured so that the file type is not hidden. Otherwise you will create files which are actually named IgorCall.bat.txt and IgorInstructions.itx.txt – these are not the file types which are required.
2. Adapt the paths in the code below to your system.

Usage:

Execute the batch file IgorCall.bat with a double-click.

Code:

Batch file (name: IgorCall.bat):
```
start Igor.exe IgorInstructions.itx
exit
```

Igor-text file (name: IgorInstructions.itx):
```
IGOR
WAVES /D 'dataset_1'
BEGIN
    1
    4
    9
    16
```

Sample Programs

```
END
X NewPath OutPutDir "C:Users:Admin:Desktop"
X variable /G refout=0
X Open /P=OutPutDir refout as "OSops.bat"
X fprintf refout, "cd C:/Users/Admin/Desktop\r\n"
X fprintf refout, "mkdir TEST\r\n"
X fprintf refout, "echo hello\r\n"
X fprintf refout, "pause\r\n"
X Close refout
X executeScriptText "\"C:\\Users\\Admin\\Desktop\\OSops.bat\""
X NewPath SaveDir "C:Users:Admin:Desktop:Test"
X Display 'dataset_1'
X SavePICT/E=-5/B=72 /P=SaveDir /O
X quit()
```

Sample Programs

8.14 Using a hook function when closing a window

Idea:

The term *hook function* and the concept of hooking are also known in other programming languages. In general, a hook function is used to intercept and modify a function call that goes directly to another function, application, or to the operating system. In this example, the click on the "x-button" to close a panel is intercepted by a window hook function. This window hook function then executes further instructions; here, the deletion of a global variable.

Usage:

Execute GuiHook#main() from the command line.

Code:

```
#pragma moduleName = GUIHook

static function main()

    variable /G root:value = 1    //create a global object

    NewPanel /K=1 /W=(75,45,418,257) /N=TestPanel
    //install window hook
    SetWindow TestPanel, hook(ArbitraryHookName)=GUIHook#MyHook

end


static function MyHook(s)

    STRUCT WMWinHookStruct &s      //one of Igor's pre-defined structures
    variable hookInfo = 0          //not mandatory, but useful for internal reasons

    switch(s.eventCode)
        case 2:                    // kill event, see Igor manual for further codes
            print "Cleaning up"
            KillVariables /Z root:value    //remove the global object
            hookInfo = 1
        break

    endswitch
    return hookInfo

end
```

Sample Programs

8.15 Using function references

Idea:

Function references can be used to tell a function which other function to call. This becomes very useful if there are many alternative functions. In this case, using a function reference helps to avoid lengthy decision structures.

Usage:

Try several function calls:
- FRefDemo#FlexMain(4, "FRefDemo#no1")
- FRefDemo#FlexMain(3, "FRefDemo#no2")
- FRefDemo#FlexMain(5, "FRefDemo#no5")
- FRefDemo#FlexMain(5, "SomethingNotThere")
- etc.

Code:

```
#pragma moduleName = FRefDemo

//----- BEWARE OF NAME CONFLICTS

function PrototypeFunc(a)              //this must NOT be static!

    variable a

    // This function definition serves as
    // a) a blue print for the compiler, specifying the
    //    function type (number parameters) of the referenced functions
    // b) a default function which is executed if the program
    //    receives an invalid reference

    print "The function that you wanted to use does not exist!"
end

//----- A large number of functions
//----- The more alternative functions there are, the more useful FuncRef becomes

static function no1(variable a)        //C like inline declaration to keep the code short
    return a
end


static function no2(variable a)
    return a^2
end
```

Sample Programs

```
static function no3(variable a)
    return sqrt(a)
end


static function no4(variable a)
    return sin(a)
end


static function no5(variable a)
    return cos(a)
end


static function no6(variable a)
    return tan(a)
end


//----- main routine

static function FlexMain(variable a, string funcName)

    FuncRef PrototypeFunc fin=$funcName
    print fin(a)

    // Imagine you would have not only 6, but 20 or more alternative functions.
    // Without FuncRef, you would have to make a decision structure
    // (e.g., strswitch) with 20 different choices!  A lot of code.
    // FuncRef makes the code much shorter.

end
```

Sample Programs

8.16 A simple neural network for curve fitting

Idea:

Igor natively supports neural networks and we will take advantage of this to implement a curve fitting algorithm. (You would not expect that the neural network would find the optimal fit like a gradient-descent method – but you can expect it to recognize the shape of the curve and find a reasonable approximation.) In the program we have to normalize the x and y ranges to the interval between 0 and 1 (this is a requirement of Igor's built in neural network), and to keep it simple we assume that the points in all test curves are equally spaced and always at the same x positions.

For more complex fits (more parameters), the internal settings of the neural network will have to be adapted during the teaching stage. This can be quite complex, however, the example below will get you started. For more information see the help on NeuralNetworkTrain and NeuralNetworkRun.

General information about neural networks is abundantly available online.

Usage:
1. Start to train the neural network with the command: NeuNet#teach(150) (the parameter controls the number of training sets – too few or too many can influence if the neural network training is successful or not)
2. Run the program: NeuNet#run()
3. Visualize the result: NeuNet#show()
4. Repeat NeuNet#run() for a couple of times and observe the results

Code:

```
#pragma moduleName = NeuNet

static constant N =70
static constant low = 0
static constant high = 1
static constant width = 0.01


static function teach(M)

	variable M              // number of parameter sets for training
	variable i

	make /o/d/n=(M,2) TrainingParameters
```

Sample Programs

```
    wave par = TrainingParameters

    // for simplicity, use random parameters in a reasonable range
    // first column: amplitude
    // second column: position
    // then, each row contains a full parameter set
    par[][0]=0.1 + 0.8*(0.5+enoise(0.5))        //[0.1 ; 0.9]
    par[][1]=0.5 + enoise(0.45)                 //[0.05 ; 0.95]

    // generate the curves of the training parameters
    make /o/d/n=(M,N) TrainingCurves
    wave tc = TrainingCurves
    SetScale /l y, low, high, tc                // note the normalization to [0,1]

    // store them in rows, not in columns
    for (i=0; i<M; i+=1)
        tc[i][] = par[i][0]*exp(-(y-par[i][1])^2/width)
    endfor

    //now the neural network will learn the
    //connection between parameters and curveshape

    NeuralNetworkTrain nhidden=50, input=tc ,output=par

    // the result of this learning process will be saved in two
    //waves M_weights1 and M_weights2
    // these waves contain all the necessary information for running the network

end


static function run()

    // ------------
    // make an arbitrary test curve
    make /o/d/n=(N) sampleWave          // number of points has to be the same as
                                        // in the training set!
    wave sW = sampleWave
    SetScale /l x,low,high, sW

    // neural networks are better with interpolating rather then extrapolating:
    // use smaller ranges than in the training set
    variable randomHeight = 0.2 + 0.6*(0.5+enoise(0.5))    //[0.2 ; 0.8]
    variable randomLoc = 0.5 + enoise(0.25)                //[0.25 ; 0.75]

    sW = randomHeight*exp(-(x-randomLoc)^2/width)
    sw += gnoise(0.01)
```

Sample Programs

```
	// ------------
	// make references to the output waves of the training session
	wave W1 = M_weights1
	wave W2 = M_weights2
	
	// run the neural network
	NeuralNetworkRun input=sW, weightsWave1=W1, weightsWave2=W2
	
	// ------------
	// draw the result
	// the wave W_NNResults is automatically created by the neural network
	wave NNRes = W_NNResults
	
	make /D /O /N=(N) NNCurve
	wave NNC = NNCurve
	SetScale /I x,low, high, NNC
	
	NNC = NNRes[0]*exp(-(x-NNRes[1])^2/width)

end


static function show()

	// call this function only after NeuNet#run() was active at least once
	// so all waves are actually there
	
	wave sW = sampleWave
	wave NNC = NNCurve
	
	Display sW
	AppendToGraph NNC

end
```

Appendix A   GUI Control Elements

The following table summarizes the patterns for control element function definitions. The procedure subtype specifiers (e.g., ButtonControl) have been omitted because they are not mandatory. See "procedure subtypes" in the Igor manual for further information.

Control element	Corresponding control function and function subtype specifier
Button	ButtonControl

Old style	function *procName*(ctrlName)
	   string ctrlName
	
	   return 0
	end

New style	function *ActionProcName*(B_Struct)
	   STRUCT WMButtonAction &B_Struct
	
	   return 0
	end

Check box	CheckBoxControl

Old style	Function *procName*(ctrlName,checked)
	   String ctrlName
	   Variable checked // 1 if selected, 0 if not
	
	   return 0
	End

New style	Function *ActionProcName*(CB_Struct)
	   STRUCT WMCheckboxAction &CB_Struct
	
	   return 0
	End

Set variable	SetVariableControl

Old style	function *procName*(ctrlName,varNum,varStr,varName)
	  String ctrlName
	  Variable varNum // value of variable as number
	  String varStr // value of variable as string
	  String varName // name of variable
	
	  return 0
	End

New style	Function *ActionProcName*(SV_Struct)
	  STRUCT WMSetVariableAction &SV_Struct
	
	  return 0
	End

Pop-up menu	PopupMenuControl

Old style	Function PopupMenuAction(ctrlName,popNum,popStr)
	  String ctrlName
	  Variable popNum // which item is currently selected
	                        //(1-based)
	  String popStr // contents of current popup
	                        //item as string
	  return 0
	End

New style	Function PopupMenuAction(PU_Struct)
	  STRUCT WMPopupAction &PU_Struct
	
	  return 0
	End

List box	ListBoxControl

Old style	Function MyListboxProc(ctrlName,row,col,event)
	  String ctrlName // name of this control
	  Variable row // row number
	  Variable col // column number
	  Variable event // event code
	
	  return 0
	End

New style	Function ListBoxProc(LB_Struct)
	  STRUCT WMListboxAction &LB_Struct
	
	  return 0
	End

Slider	SliderControl

Old style	Function MySliderProc(ctrlName, value, event)
	  String ctrlName // name of this slider control
	  Variable value // value of slider
	  Variable event // bit field:bit 0:value set;
	                 // 1:mouse down,
	                 // 2:mouse up,
	                 // 3:mouse moved
	  return 0
	End

New style	Function *ActionProcName*(S_Struct)
	  STRUCT WMSliderAction &S_Struct
	
	  return 0
	End

Tab control	TabControl

Old style	Function ManageTabs(ctrlName,tab)
	  String ctrlName
	  Variable tab
	
	  return 0
	End

New style	Function *ActionProcName*(TC_Struct)
	  STRUCT WMTabControlAction &TC_Struct
	
	  return 0
	End

The new-style type uses the built-in structure definitions for the various control elements. In addition to the control elements above, Igor allows to generate user-defined control elements: custom controls. They can be similarly controlled as the regular control elements. The corresponding built-in-structure is WMCustomControlAction.

Appendix B   List box modes and bit parameters

A *list box* (created by the command ListBox) is a very versatile, but also somewhat tricky, control element for graphical user interfaces. You can think of a list box as a sophisticated form of table.

- A list box is a display element for a one or two-dimensional text wave. This text wave is usually referred to as the "listWave" of the list box.

- It is possible to control/customize individual cells in the table. The necessary meta-information about the cells in the table is saved in a separate numeric wave, which is usually referred to as "selWave". The entries in the selWave control, for instance, if cells are editable, contain checkbox elements (yes, this feature is built into the list box), but also the color of individual cells and the color of the fonts in the cell.

- Both waves associated with the list box must have the same number of rows and columns. The selWave can have additional layers, which are usually used to control font and background color in the list box.

- When the user interacts with the list box, i.e., selects or edits cells, a *list box procedure function* can receive specific signals that can be used to trigger events. For example: if a list box contains a list with the waves in the current data folder, selecting a cell with a wave name could trigger the creation of a graph with this specific wave.

It is important to be aware that selecting cells and editing cells are two different things! The way by which cells are *selectable* is defined in the list box definition in the code with the keyword mode. mode can take values from 0 to 10.

The decision if a selected cell is *editable* as well is defined as meta-information in the selWave! This meta-information is encoded in bit parameters, i.e., binary sequences like 0000100. The entries in the selWave are not the direct binary control variables, but their corresponding decimal representations. The bit count starts with bit 0 at the right side of the binary sequence:

Bit index	6 5 4 3 2 1 0
Bit parameter (example)	1 0 1 0 1 1 0

Each bit has a meaning, e.g., setting bit 1 makes a cell editable: in this case, the binary sequence is 0000010 and the selWave displays 2. If an editable cell was highlighted with a *Shift-click* (pressing the shift key on the keyboard and clicking into the cell, setting bit 3 with mode=10), the result is 0001010 – which is displayed in its decimal representation as 10.

A further example: If a cell in selWave displays the value 9 (with mode=10, after marking a cell which was first marked with a *Ctrl-click* with an additional *Shift-click*), the bit parameter is set to 0001001. Bit 0 and bit 3 are set at the same time set to 1. Bit 0 from the *Ctrl-click* and bit 3 from the subsequent *Shift-click*.

The combinations of modes and bits can be very confusing!

The following program can be used to become familiar with the selection behavior with different modes and bits. The embedded table allows to observe the selWave entries and how they change. The modes can take values from 0 to 10; call the program from the command line, e.g., with: listBoxPlayground#modes(m=10). Here is the code:

```
#pragma moduleName = listBoxPlayground

static function modes([m]) : Panel

    variable m
    m = (ParamIsDefault(m)? 0 : m)

    //only one instance allowed
    DoWindow ListPanel
    if (V_Flag)
        DoWindow /K ListPanel        //kill the old instance
    endif

    string caption = "Panel with listbox in mode: " + num2str(m)
    NewPanel /K=1 /N=ListPanel /W=(75,45,768,314) as caption

    make /T /N=(5,3) /O List
    wave /T List=List

    make /D /N=(5,3) /O Sel
    wave Sel = Sel
```

136

```
Sel = 0x00    //without this initialization one can observe
              //memory effects between different runs of the program
              //The /O flag in the make command does not erase
              //all information as one would expect
              // PLAY WITH THIS VALUE

ListBox LB1,pos={7.50,7.00},size={348.00,255.50}
ListBox LB1,listWave=List, selWave= Sel, mode=(m)

//also show the entries for the meta-information
Edit/W=(364,7,688,259)/HOST=# Sel      // /Host=# subwindow assignment

ModifyTable format(Point)=1
RenameWindow #,SelTable                // # again for subwindow assignment
SetActiveSubwindow ##

end
```

The listbox behaves like a regular spreadsheet with `mode=10`. Initialize the selwave with different values and observe the effects — 0x20 and 0x40 have interesting effects.

Appendix C   Igor vs. other languages

For comparison, a simple hello world program is listed here along with its counterparts in C, C++, and Java.

Igor (module-static approach)
```
#pragma moduleName = HelloWorld
static function main()
    print "Hello World"
end
```

C
```
#include<stdio.h>
main(){
   printf("Hello World");
   return 0;
   }
```

C++
```
#include <iostream>
using namespace std;
int main(){
    cout << "Hello, World";
    return 0;
    }
```

Java
```
class HelloWorldProg {
   public static void main(String[] args) {
     System.out.println("Hello World");
     }
   }
```

How are name conflicts prevented in each case? In Igor, using the module-static approach is enough. In C, only one function per code-file can have the name main(), trying otherwise gives a compilation error. In C++ the situation is similar to C, however the namespace is additionally set to "std". In Java the main function of the class "HelloWorldProg" is encapsulated in the function definition.

If one follows the module-static approach, Igor Pro code can look structurally similar to code written in other programming languages.

The syntax of the Igor program is relatively simple and straightforward if compared to C++ or Java: there are significantly fewer special characters part of the syntax. On the other hand, it is not possible to create executables (.exe) from Igor code – the programs cannot run independently from Igor Pro. And while the module-static approach allows to generate reusable, encapsulated code, Igor Pro does not allow full object oriented programming.

Appendix D Function declarations

| No return value, no parameters | ```
function foo()
    //code
end
``` |
| Variable return value, no parameters | ```
function foo()
    variable a = 2
    //code
    return a
end
``` |
| Complex return value, no parameters | ```
function /C foo()
    variable /C p=cmplx(1,2)
    //code
    return p
end
``` |
| Multiple return values (Igor 8) | ```
function [ Variable v, String s ] foo( )
    return [2, "hello world"]
end

... // receiving values in another function
    [a,word] = foo ()
....
``` |
| String return value, no parameters | ```
function /S foo()
    string s=""
    //code
    return s
end
``` |
| Data folder reference return value, no parameters | ```
function /DF foo()
    DFREF DFref = GetDataFolderDFR()
    return DFref
end
``` |

Wave reference return value, no parameters	function /WAVE foo()
	    make /D /O example
	    wave test = example
	
	    return test
	end

No return value, parameters by value (optional parameter c)	function foo(a,s,[c])
	    variable a
	    string s
	    variable c
	end

No return value, parameters by reference	function foo(a,s)
	    variable &a
	    string &s
	
	end

No return value, structure parameter	function foo(st)
	    struct &st
	    //code
	end

No return value, wave reference parameter	function foo(W)
	    wave W
	    //code
	end

No return value, data folder reference parameter:	function foo(location)
	    DFREF location
	    //code
	end

Appendix E   Useful keyboard shortcuts

Particularly useful shortcuts are highlighted in **bold font**. Some very common shortcuts, such as Ctrl+O for opening another file, or Ctrl+C and Ctrl+V for copy and paste, are not mentioned here. These very common operations are accessible via the menu bar and the shortcuts are indicated there as well. On Mac computers, Ctrl is substituted by Cmd and Alt by Option. There can be variations between different Igor versions.

Shortcut	Action
Ctrl+D	Duplicate a graph or a marked wave
Ctrl+I	Set cursors on a graph
Ctrl+W	Close top window
Ctrl+Alt+W	Close without asking
Ctrl+Shift+W	Hide window
Ctrl+B	Call data browser
Ctrl+T	Activate the tool palette for a window
Ctrl+Z	Undo
Ctrl+Shift+Z	Redo
Ctrl+K	Clear command line
Ctrl+A	Autoscale axes
Ctrl+Enter	Execute code in an Igor help file
Ctrl+J	Go to command line
Ctrl+M	Go to procedure window
Ctrl+Shift+M	Cycle through procedure windows
Ctrl+Y	Window control dialog
Ctrl+E	Cycle through the windows in the experiment
Ctrl+Shift+E	Change direction of Ctrl+E

Ctrl+F	Find
Ctrl+G	Find next
Ctrl+Shift+G	Find previous
Ctrl+R	Find and replace text
Ctrl+S	Save experiment
Ctrl+Shift+S	Save a (procedure) window
Ctrl+/ (procedure window)	Commentize code segments
Ctrl+ (procedure window)	Decommentize code segments
Ctrl+Shift+L (in procedure window)	Indent left (apply to code segments)
Ctrl+Shift+R (in procedure window)	Indent right (apply to code segments)
Ctrl+I (in procedure window)	Adjust indentation of code segments

Shortcuts for finding help

Shortcut	Action
F1	Call help browser.
Ctrl+Alt+F1	Help for selection. Example: enter print on the command line, highlight it with the mouse (print), and use the shortcut. Note: putting the cursor into the command counts as highlighting as well.
Ctrl+Alt+T	Insert template for selection. Example: enter print on the command line, highlight it with the mouse (print), and use the shortcut.
Ctrl+Alt+B (Igor 7)	Show the previously displayed help topic.

Index

#

for subwindow syntax ... 118, 135
#include statements 13
#pragma
    moduleName 11
    rtGlobals 6
    TextEncoding 6

A

accessing the hard drive 85, 88, 106, 124
array 53
    local 57

B

bit operators 83
bit parameters 82, 135
break 46

C

characters
    ASCII 67
    unicode 67
    UTF-8, UTF-16 67
code encapsulation 14, 138
code layout 7
coding style 7
command line 2
compiler directives .... *See* #
complex
    constants 62
    variable 29
    wave 55
constants 62
continue 50
conversion

decimal-octal, decimal-hex, decimal-binary See formatted printing
    string to name 38
    variable-string 32

D

datafolders 62
debugger 6
dependency 65
do-while loop 48

E

encapsulation 14
error handling 90

F

for loop 48
formatted printing 76
    sprintf 73
    wfprintf 75
formula .... *See* dependency
functions 27
    declarations, reference table 140
    hook functions 126
    optional parameters 41, 42
    pass-by-reference 41
    pass-by-value 41
    static 12, 27

G

global data-objects 52
graphical user interfaces 15
    list box 135

H

help files 88

I

if-else 45
    elseif 46
implicit
    references 38
    variables 35
INF 31

K

keyboard shortcuts 142

M

make I/O memory effect 61
measuring time 97
module-static approach 10, 138

N

name conflicts 138
NaN 31, 91

O

operators
    bitwise 83
    global strings 37
    global variables 37
    local strings 32
    local variables 29
    waves 37

P

paths 66, 86
procedure subtypes 27
procedure window 2

R

random numbers 108
references
    from graphs 40
    implicit 38
    to global objects 36
regular expressions 78, 115
    character classes 80

S

sharing code 14
strings 31, 66
    conversion 32, 70
    escape sequences 73
    key-value lists 75
    list strings 74
    operations with 68
    sprintf 73
    sscanf 71
strswitch-case 46
structures 33
    for GUI control elements 118, 132
subroutines 7
subwindow syntax 118, 135
switch-case 46

V

variables 28
    complex 28
    conversion 32

W

waves 53
    accuracy 55
    different types of 55
    multidimensional 57

Printed in Great Britain
by Amazon